Editorial Project Manager
Erica N. Russikoff, M.A.

Editor in Chief
Karen J. Goldfluss, M.S. Ed.

Creative Director
Sarah M. Fournier

Cover Artist
Sarah Kim

Imaging
Amanda R. Harter

Publisher
Mary D. Smith, M.S. Ed.

TCR 8253

LET'S GET THIS 3
DAY STARTED
Writing and Language Skills

- Start the day off right with engaging, standards-based writing, grammar, and language activities.

- Comprehensive three-page units focus on essential language skills.

- Each unit has a unique, specific theme, which serves as a basis for whole-group, small-group, and partner activities.

- Activities may include photographs, which provide a real-life connection for learning.

Teacher Created Resources

Author
Tracie I. Heskett, M. Ed.

Teacher Created Resources
12621 Western Avenue
Garden Grove, CA 92841
www.teachercreated.com
ISBN: 978-1-4206-8253-3
© 2019 Teacher Created Resources
Made in U.S.A.

Teacher Created Resources

Table of Contents

Introduction

Writing and language skills help us communicate with one another. Students need guidance, assistance, and practice to develop these particular skills. *Let's Get This Day Started: Writing and Language Skills* explicitly teaches specific writing and grammar concepts as well as language skills. In a diverse society, students do not always have opportunities to hear and learn English from seeing and hearing language used correctly in context. In addition, language and its use change as new technology impacts the ways in which people communicate. We are all English learners, whether as native speakers or second-language novices. Explicit language instruction helps students acquire specific skills that contribute positively to their academic learning and effective communication with others.

There are two main sections in this book. In both sections, students will practice grammar and language skills with peers in whole-group, small-group, and partner settings and then apply it to their own writing.

The first part teaches grammar and writing skills that enable students to write more effectively. The goal of effective writing is to engage readers in such a way that they comprehend and respond to what they read. In these units, students study how correct use of grammar results in effective writing.

The second part introduces vocabulary skills, including figurative language. These skills encourage students to use grade-level-appropriate general-academic and domain-specific vocabulary in their reading, writing, speaking, and listening. Vocabulary skills help students better understand how language works in a variety of contexts. As they practice and develop these skills, students grasp differences in style and meaning to increase their reading and listening comprehension, as well as writing abilities.

Each unit presents the focus concept to students through explanation, examples, and activities. The concepts presented generally follow the scope and sequence of the Common Core State Standards Initiative, which seeks to provide students with the knowledge and skills they need to be successful in college, career, and life.

Activities within each unit focus on a specific theme. Students will write about grade-level-appropriate, relevant topics of interest. These topics were gathered from current news and events, popular culture, and themes in child development.

The skills covered in *Let's Get This Day Started: Writing and Language Skills* are used and needed every day. Help your children or students master these skills as they will use them throughout the rest of their educational careers and lives.

How to Use This Book

Each unit has three sections. The first is *Learn*, a lesson page addressed to students. This page introduces a grammar, writing, or language skill through observation and activities designed to engage students. Any new, related vocabulary is also introduced. In many cases, students participate in a whole-class activity during this part of the lesson. These activities provide scaffolding and support for students as they begin their initial practice of the skill.

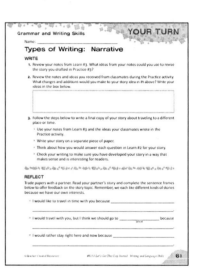

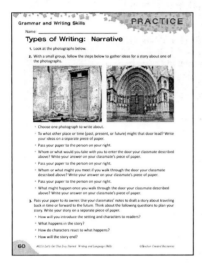

Practice continues in the second part of the lesson. Students work collaboratively in whole-group, small-group, or partner activities, which give them continued guidance and support.

The third page in each unit, *Your Turn*, has two parts: *Write* and *Reflect*. *Your Turn* presents one or more writing prompts for students to practice the skill independently. After students incorporate the skill into their writing, they reflect on their learning individually or with a partner. The reflection activity provides students with the opportunity to review, confirm, and reinforce their learning and its application in their writing. The additional practice and implementation will help them remember what they have learned.

Some units incorporate photographs in student activities. These add a realistic element to the writing prompts and engage students by providing a real-life connection for their learning. When making photocopies of activity pages, it is best to use the photo setting so the images are easier to see. You may wish to supplement other activities with related photographs or other visual aids. Plan to preview each lesson; some units include a teacher icon. This icon ![] indicates that the lesson needs additional teacher preparation.

Answers for some of the units in this book can be found in the Answer Key on pages 107–109. In addition to specific answers for some student activities, the Answer Key also provides suggested answers for some of the teacher-led (icon) activities.

All of the activities in the *Let's Get This Day Started* series have been aligned to the Common Core State Standards (CCSS). A correlations chart is included on pages 110–112.

Name: _____

Nouns: Plural, Regular and Irregular

> **Plural nouns** name more than one person, place, or thing. Usually we make a noun plural by adding -*s* or -*es*.
>
> Examples: apples, sandwiches, tomatoes

> **Irregular plural nouns** don't always follow this rule. Sometimes, we have to change one or more letters.
>
> Examples: berry → berries, calf → calves
>
> Some nouns take a different form in the plural than in the singular.
>
> Examples: child → children, tooth → teeth
>
> Some nouns keep the same form for both plural and singular.
>
> Examples: cod → cod, sheep → sheep

1. Look at the photographs below. Write the plural form of the noun that names each set of objects on the line below each picture.

_____   _____

2. Think about the correct form of a plural noun to complete the sentences below.

   (a) Three _____ of bread were cooling at the bakery.

   (b) The chef washed several _____ of lettuce to make a salad.

3. Think about how to form the plural in the following examples.

   (a) Some people now make hamburgers out of bison. Write a sentence to state that someone saw more than one bison in a field. Use a separate piece of paper.

   (b) Cherry season lasts only a short time in early summer. Write a sentence to describe how you could eat more than one of this fruit. Use the same separate piece of paper.

Name: _____

Nouns: Plural, Regular and Irregular

1. Work with a small group to answer the questions below. You will write a recipe to prepare a certain food or dish.

▪ Talk about foods you know how to prepare or dishes you know how to make. Which one will you write a recipe for?

_____

▪ What ingredients do you need to make this food or dish? Often, a recipe lists ingredients in the order they are used.

_____

_____

_____

▪ What steps will you follow to make this food or dish? Write the directions in an order that makes sense.

_____

_____

_____

_____

_____

_____

▪ What other foods do people often eat with this food or dish?

_____

_____

2. Share your recipe with the class. Talk about the questions below.

▪ How did you use plural nouns in your recipe?

▪ Which foods or ingredients do we often eat in their plural form (for example, grapes)?

▪ Who might enjoy eating the food or dish prepared from your recipe? Why?

YOUR TURN

Name: _____

Nouns: Plural, Regular and Irregular

WRITE

1. Think about your favorite foods and list them below. Use the correct plural forms of nouns as needed.

_____

_____

_____

_____

2. When do you eat these foods?

_____

_____

_____

3. What other foods do you often eat with these favorite foods?

_____

_____

_____

4. Write a journal entry to describe your favorite foods. Use your notes from answering the questions above. Write your journal entry on a separate piece of paper.

REFLECT

1. Answer the questions below with a partner to compare your favorite foods.
   - Are there any foods you both enjoy?
   - How are your favorite foods similar?
   - How are your favorite foods different?
   - Which foods do you usually eat more than one of (in its plural form)? Why?

2. Draw a Venn diagram to show the results of your discussion. Label the circles with your names to show who likes which foods. Use a separate piece of paper.

Name: _____

Pronouns: Subject and Object

A **pronoun** is a word used in place of a noun. A pronoun may name a person, a place, a thing, or an idea. We use pronouns in different ways in sentences.

We use a **subject pronoun** as the subject of a sentence. It names who or what is doing the action. Subject pronouns are *I, you, he, she, it, we, you,* and *they.*

Example: The <u>students</u> wrote letters on Veterans Day.

 <u>They</u> wrote letters on Veterans Day.

We use an **object pronoun** after an action verb. It names who or what is receiving the action. Object pronouns are *me, you, him, her, it, us, you,* and *them.*

Example: The class asked the <u>soldier</u> questions.
 The class asked <u>him</u> questions.

The form of a pronoun we use depends on how it is used in a sentence.

Example: Caleb and <u>I</u> watched the Veterans Day parade.

 I is a subject in this sentence. We use the subject form of the pronoun.

Example: Mom gave Caleb and <u>me</u> flags to wave.

 Me is the object of the action *gave*. We use the object form of the pronoun.

These examples have more than one subject. If you are not sure which form of a pronoun to use, read the example with only one subject at a time.

Example: <u>I</u> watched the Veterans Day parade.

 I is the correct form of the pronoun. (We would not say, "*Me* watched the Veterans Day parade.")

Example: Mom gave <u>me</u> a flag to wave.

 Me is the correct form of the pronoun. (We would not say, "Mom gave *I* a flag to wave.")

1. Use the information given above to make a pronoun chart with classmates. Answer the questions below to think about how to set up your chart. Write your chart on chart paper or a whiteboard.
    - Which pronouns are singular?
    - Which pronouns are plural?
    - How might you group the pronouns?

2. Follow the directions below to write sample sentences with classmates about things you do on holidays. Use a separate piece of paper.
    - Use pronouns in your sentences.
    - Use the chart you made for #1 to help you write your sentences.

Name: _____

Pronouns: Subject and Object

1. Work with a small group to read about a veteran or famous person connected with a holiday. Your teacher may help you think of and research someone. ⚠

2. Complete the graphic organizer on the right.

3. Write the name of the person in the oval.

4. Answer the questions below to complete the graphic organizer.

- Why is this person famous or respected? Write your answers in the "Character Qualities" spaces.

- What has this person said that shows their character qualities? Write your answers in the "Words" spaces.

- What did this person do that benefits others in some way? Write your answers in the "Actions" spaces.

5. Follow the steps below to write sentences about the person you researched. Use a separate piece of paper.

- Work together to write an informative paragraph.

- Think about actions the person did and who or what received the actions.

- Include subject and object pronouns in your sentences.

6. Introduce to classmates the person your group researched by sharing your paragraph.

7. Ask and answer questions about classmates' paragraphs. Practice using pronouns in your question and answer sentences.

Character Qualities

Words

Actions

YOUR TURN

Name: _____

Pronouns: Subject and Object

WRITE

1. Write questions to ask a classmate about their favorite holiday.

_____

_____

_____

_____

_____

2. Ask your partner the questions. Write their answers below.

_____

_____

_____

_____

_____

_____

REFLECT

1. Trade papers with a different partner. Which nouns in your partner's sentences from #2 above could you replace with pronouns? Rewrite the sentences on a separate piece of paper.

2. Talk with your partner about the questions below.

- What different kinds of pronouns did you study in this lesson?

- What do pronouns do in sentences?

- Why do we use pronouns?

Grammar and Writing Skills

Name: _____

Verbs: Simple Past, Present, and Future

Verbs show action. They also tell when something happened.

A **past tense verb** states an action that happened in the past. We form many regular past tense verbs by adding *-ed* to the verb.

A **present tense verb** tells about something that is happening now. It may be an action that happens regularly.

A **future tense verb** states an action that will happen later, or in the future. We use the word *will* or *shall* before the verb to make it future tense. The words *will* and *shall* are helping verbs.

1. What actions do people do when they play indoor sports? Write your ideas on a separate piece of paper.

2. Follow the directions below to make word cards.

   ▪ Choose one verb from your list in #1 above. Write the word "past" and the past tense form of the verb on a slip of paper.

   ▪ Choose a different verb from your list. Write the word "present" and the present tense form of the verb on a different slip of paper.

   ▪ Choose another verb from your list. Write the word "future" and the future tense form of the verb on another slip of paper.

   ▪ Follow the three steps above to make more word cards.

   ▪ Fold each slip of paper in half. Your teacher will have you write an "X" (or an "O") on the outside of each folded slip of paper. 🔰

3. Work with a partner to draw a tic-tac-toe grid on a separate piece of paper.

4. Follow the directions below to play a game of tic-tac-toe with your partner.

   ▪ Take turns placing one of your folded paper slips on the grid, with your "X" or "O" mark facing up.

   ▪ Place a different verb tense card on the game board each turn.

   ▪ The first person to cover three spaces in a row with their mark is the "master" for this game. Together, check your word cards to make sure all of the verb tenses are correct.

5. If you have time, play another game with a different partner. Use a different set of word cards.

©*Teacher Created Resources*   *#8253 Let's Get This Day Started: Writing and Language Skills*   **11**

PRACTICE

Name: _____

Verbs: Simple Past, Present, and Future

1. Work with a small group. Answer the questions below to plan a board game.

   ▪ What is the main idea for your game? What fun theme will you have for your game?

   _____

   _____

   ▪ What are some things players might have to do when they draw a card?

   _____

   _____

   ▪ What supplies will you need to play your game (for example, game pieces and dice)?

   _____

   _____

2. Follow the steps below to make your group's board game.

   ▪ Draw a game board on a separate piece of paper or cardstock.

   ▪ Include a space to start and a space to finish.

   ▪ Mark some spaces on your game board for players to draw a card.

   ▪ Review your answers to the questions in #1 above.

   ▪ Work together to write game cards. Each person in your group might write two or three game cards. Include past, present, and future verbs when you write your cards. Do not underline the verbs.

   Examples:

   You <u>stepped</u> in a mud hole. Go back two spaces.

   You <u>play</u> well with friends. Skip ahead to the smiley face.

   It <u>will rain</u> soon. Run ahead one space to the tree to stay dry.

   ▪ Write directions to tell people how to play your game.

   ▪ Decorate your game board with colorful pictures and neat lettering.

3. Trade games (board, game cards, and playing directions) with another group.

4. Read the cards your classmates made for their game. Underline any past, present, and future verbs they used. Did they use the verb tenses correctly?

5. If you have time, play the game your classmates made.

YOUR TURN

Name: _____

Verbs: Simple Past, Present, and Future

WRITE

1. Answer the questions below to think about an experience you had playing your favorite game or indoor sport. Write your answers in complete sentences.

   ▪ What actions did you do when you played the game or sport? Use past tense verbs.

   _____

   _____

   ▪ What actions do you do every time you play this game or sport? Use present tense verbs.

   _____

   _____

   ▪ What actions would you do differently or better the next time you play this game or sport? Use future tense verbs.

   _____

   _____

2. Use your answers to the questions above to write a narrative about your experience. Use past, present, and future verb tenses correctly in your writing. Write your narrative on a separate piece of paper.

REFLECT

1. Make a verb tense color key. Use a different-colored pencil or crayon to color the box next to each verb tense below.

   ☐ past tense   ☐ present tense   ☐ future tense

2. Read a classmate's narrative. Follow the steps below to review how your classmate used verb tenses.

   ▪ Use the verb tense color key you made in #1 above.

   ▪ Highlight each verb with the correct color to show the verb tense.

3. Answer the questions below with your partner.

   ▪ What do you notice about how your partner used different verb tenses?

   ▪ How did the verbs your partner used show when things happened in the narrative?

   ▪ What have you learned in this lesson about the different verb tenses?

Name: _____

Subject-Verb Agreement

The parts of a sentence must agree with one another. We call this **subject-verb agreement**. If a sentence has a singular subject, it must also have a singular verb. If a sentence has a plural subject, it must also have a plural verb. We do this so readers or listeners know that the subject and the verb in a sentence are talking about the same number of people or things.

Examples: A <u>bear</u> <u>hunts</u> for food.

The sentence talks about one bear. *Hunts* is the singular form of the verb.

<u>Bears</u> <u>hunt</u> for food.

The sentence talks about more than one bear. *Hunt* is the plural form of the verb.

1. Follow the directions below to mark the sentences in #2.
   - Underline the subject in each sentence.
   - Write the number "1" or "2+" above each subject to show how many people, places, things, or ideas the sentence describes.
   - Draw a box around the verb in each sentence.
   - Write the letter "S" or "P" above the verb to show whether it is the singular or plural form of the verb.

2. Read the sentences below and mark each sentence as directed in #1 above.

   - We study animals at school.

   - California condors have a huge wingspan.

   - Their wings are 8 to 10 feet long.

   - The Chinese giant salamander is the largest amphibian in the world.

   - It weighs as much as 110 pounds.

   - The monkeys and baboons live in a new habitat.

3. Write one or two sentences about animals. Make sure the verb matches the subject in number. Write your sentences on a separate piece of paper.

4. Share your sentence(s) with classmates.

5. Talk about what you noticed about subject-verb agreement in the sample sentences in #2 above.

PRACTICE

Name: _____

Subject-Verb Agreement

1. Work with a small group to make word cards. Write subjects and verbs on slips of paper. Write each subject and verb on a separate card. A subject names who or what does the action in a sentence. A verb states the action the subject does. Remember, a subject may be singular or plural, or have more than one part, connected by the word *and* or *or*.

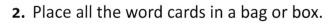

2. Place all the word cards in a bag or box.

3. Trade your bag or box with another small group.

4. Take turns following the steps below to play a grab-bag game.

   - Draw two cards from the bag.

   - If you have a subject and a verb, write a sentence. Make sure your subject and verb agree in number. Use a separate piece of paper.

   - If you do not have a subject and a verb or if your subject and verb do not agree in number, hold on to your word cards.

   - On your next turn, draw two more cards. Write sentences with as many of your words as you can. Use the same separate piece of paper.

   - Continue taking turns drawing out word cards and writing sentences until you have used all of the word cards.

5. Trade your completed sentences with the group that has your word cards. Check your classmates' writing. Give them one point for every sentence that uses a subject and verb in correct agreement.

6. How many points did that group earn? Write the total in the box below.

Name: _____

Subject-Verb Agreement

WRITE

1. Research to learn about an animal of interest to you. Your teacher may supply resources. 🔔

2. Follow the steps below to write an informative paragraph about the animal you researched. If you need more writing space, use a separate piece of paper.

   - Write a sentence to introduce your topic.

   - Write sentences with details about how the animal looks and acts.

   - Make sure subjects and verbs agree in number in your sentences.

   - Write a concluding statement for your paragraph. This sentence might explain why you think this animal is interesting.

   _____

   _____

   _____

   _____

REFLECT

1. Trade papers with a partner. Draw a smiley face next to the statements below that are true of your partner's writing.

   ◯ All of the sentences with a singular subject have a singular verb.

   ◯ All of the sentences with a plural subject have a plural verb.

   ◯ All of the sentences make sense and sound natural.

2. Write a tip for your classmate about how to make sure subjects and verbs agree in their writing.

   _____

   _____

3. Share the tip you wrote with your partner and other classmates.

Name: _____

Adjectives: Comparative and Superlative

An adjective modifies, or describes, a noun. **Comparative adjectives** compare two things. Most comparative adjectives are formed by adding *-er* to the end of an adjective.

Examples: The firefighter was <u>brave</u>.

The fire chief was <u>braver</u> than the firefighter.

In the second sentence, the fire chief is being compared to the firefighter.

Superlative adjectives compare three or more things. For most superlative adjectives, add *-est* to the end of the word.

Examples: The first giant is <u>strong</u>.

The second giant is <u>stronger</u> than the first giant.

The third giant is the <u>strongest</u> of all.

These sentences compare three giants to one another.

Some comparative and superlative adjectives change form. We call these **irregular comparative** or **superlative adjectives**.

Adjective	Comparative	Superlative
good	better	best
bad	worse	worst
much, many, some	more	most
far	farther	farthest

1. Write a sentence about a superhero. Use a separate piece of paper.

2. Trade sentences with a classmate. Write a sentence that compares your superhero to your classmate's. Write the comparative form of your adjective or their adjective in your sentence. Use the same separate piece of paper.

3. Share your sentences with the class. Work with classmates to write sentences that compare your superheroes. Use comparative and superlative adjectives in your sentences. Record your sentences on chart paper or a whiteboard.

Name: _____

Adjectives: Comparative and Superlative

1. What other adjectives could you use to describe a superhero? Write your ideas in the box below.

(box)

2. Work with two other classmates to form a group of three. Follow the steps below to practice saying comparative and superlative adjectives.

- Pick a classmate to go first.
- Take turns saying an adjective you wrote in #1 above.
- The person on your left will say the comparative form of the adjective.
- Then the third person in the group will say the superlative form of the adjective.
- Start with a different person each time so that each person practices saying adjectives, comparative adjectives, and superlative adjectives.

3. Work together to write a story about superhero characters. Follow the directions below to write your story. If you need more writing space, use a separate piece of paper.

- Use adjectives from each group member to describe superheroes in the story. Use as many comparative and superlative forms of the adjectives as you can.
- Include adventure, surprise, and excitement in your story.

_____

_____

_____

_____

_____

4. Draw pictures to illustrate your story. Your drawings should show comparative and superlative qualities of the characters. Use a separate piece of paper.

5. Record or read your story aloud to share with classmates.

YOUR TURN

Name: _____

Adjectives: Comparative and Superlative

WRITE

1. Answer the questions below to think about a real-life superhero (not a cartoon character).

   ▪ What types of actions do real people do that make us think of them as superheroes?

   _____
   _____
   _____

   ▪ Who do you know that is like a superhero in some way?

   _____

   ▪ What adjectives would you use to describe this person?

   _____
   _____

   ▪ What qualities make this person different from other people?

   _____
   _____

2. Follow the steps below to write an opinion or explanatory paragraph about your superhero. Use a separate piece of paper.

   ▪ Include information about why this person is a superhero.

   ▪ Use comparative and superlative adjectives to compare this person to other things or people.

REFLECT

Trade paragraphs with a partner. Answer the questions below on a separate piece of paper.

   ▪ Why would you like to meet your partner's superhero?

   ▪ How does your hero compare to your partner's hero?

   ▪ How does your partner's hero compare to your hero?

Adverbs: Comparative and Superlative

Name: _____

An **adverb** modifies, or describes, a verb. An adverb tells *how, how often, where, when,* and *to what extent* (or *degree of* something). An adverb can compare two different things. We call these *comparative adverbs.* When comparing two things, add *-er* to the end of a single-syllable word.

Example: Ryan ran <u>fast</u> to reach the finish line.
Mia ran <u>faster</u>.

Superlative adverbs compare more than two things. When comparing more than two things, add *-est* to the end of a single-syllable word.

Example: Elijah ran the <u>fastest</u>.

Some **comparative** and **superlative adverbs** change form when comparing two or more things.

Adverb	Comparative	Superlative
well*	better	best
badly	worse	worst
little	less	least
much/many	more	most

Well is usually an adverb describing *how*; *good* is an adjective that describes a noun.

1. With classmates, talk about adverbs you know and write them on chart paper or a whiteboard.

2. Follow the directions below to play a game with classmates.
   - Use a beanbag or another small object to pass from one person to the next.
   - Sit in a circle with classmates.
   - Your teacher will set a timer (perhaps for 30 seconds) to begin play.
   - Before the first player passes the object to the next person, they must say an adverb.
   - The second player must say the comparative form of the adverb before they pass the object along.
   - The third player must say the superlative form of the adverb before passing the object along.
   - The next person starts anew with a different adverb.
   - Play until the timer buzzes. The player holding the object when the timer buzzes must say a sentence using a comparative or superlative form of an adverb.
   - Play until several players have practiced using comparative and superlative forms of adverbs.

Name: _____

Adverbs: Comparative and Superlative

1. Work with a small group to recall comparative and superlative forms of adverbs you and your classmates said in the game you played in Learn #2.

2. Write the adverbs on the lines below.

_____   _____

_____   _____

_____   _____

_____   _____

_____   _____

_____   _____

_____   _____

3. Trade papers with another small group.

4. Work with others in your group to write a review of an outdoor sporting event. A review explains how good or bad something is and why. Write your review on a separate piece of paper. Follow the tips below.

   ▪ Use the adverbs your classmates listed for ideas about which outdoor sport you might review.

   ▪ Write about a real or an imagined event.

   ▪ Answer the questions *who, what, where, when,* and *how* to write your review.

   ▪ Write sentences about what readers would find interesting about this outdoor sport.

   ▪ Include comparative and superlative adverbs in your writing.

5. Trade papers again and read the review your classmates wrote. Talk about your answers to the questions below.

   ▪ Which adverbs from your list did classmates use in their writing?

   ▪ Did they use comparative and superlative adverbs correctly?

   ▪ How did their use of adverbs make their review more interesting?

Name: _____

Adverbs: Comparative and Superlative

WRITE

1. Answer the questions below to think about your favorite outdoor sport.

   ▪ What is your favorite outdoor sport?

   _____

   ▪ What other outdoor sport could you compare to your favorite outdoor sport?

   _____

   ▪ Which adverbs might describe actions you do when you play this sport?

   _____
   | |
   | |
   | |
   _____

   ▪ How could you use adverbs to compare the two outdoor sports?

   _____

   _____

   _____

2. Use your answers to the questions above to write an opinion paragraph about your favorite outdoor sport. Use adverbs in your writing to compare your favorite sport to another outdoor sport. Write your paragraph on a separate piece of paper.

REFLECT

1. Trade papers with a partner.

2. Adverbs may describe *how* or *to what degree* something has a certain quality. Use adverbs to answer the questions below. Describe how well your partner's writing convinces you to agree with them. Look at the sample chart in the Learn activity for ideas. Write your comments on a separate piece of paper.

   ▪ What did you like best about your partner's paragraph?

   ▪ How did you partner use adverbs to describe and compare two outdoor sports?

   ▪ What could your partner work on next time to make their writing better?

3. Share your feedback with your partner. Remember to be kind and helpful.

Name: _____

Conjunctions: Coordinating

Conjunctions are words that join parts of a sentence. **Coordinating conjunctions** connect equal sentence parts, such as two words, two phrases, or two independent clauses. A coordinating conjunction combines two simple sentences (independent clauses) into one compound sentence. We do this to show the close relationship between two ideas. Often, we use a comma before a coordinating conjunction that combines two independent clauses. A variety of sentence patterns adds interest to writing and makes it flow more smoothly.

Example: The pond was full of mud *and* green slime, *yet* we were able to clean it.

Mud and green slime are two related things. They are joined by the coordinating conjunction *and*.

The pond was full of these things. We were able to clean it. These two ideas form two independent clauses. They are related. These two independent clauses are joined by the coordinating conjunction *yet*. A comma is used to connect the clauses.

The main coordinating conjunctions are *for, and, nor, but, or, yet,* and *so*. We can remember them easily by memorizing the acronym FANBOYS.

1. Read the paragraph below. Circle the coordinating conjunctions in the paragraph.

   What is slime? We use this term to talk about anything that is moist and slippery or sticky. One plant we often describe this way is algae. Algae has a smooth, wet surface that is slippery. Algae lives in places with other plants and animals. It plays an important role in nature, but everything else must be in balance for it to be helpful.

2. What do you notice about how conjunctions are used in the paragraph above? Share your observations with classmates.

3. Work with classmates to create a poster. Follow the steps below.

   ▪ Research to learn the meaning and use of each coordinating conjunction listed in the paragraph above. Your teacher may supply resources. ⚠

   ▪ Write the words and definitions on chart paper or cardstock to create your poster. Use color and other graphics to make the poster interesting and eye-catching.

   ▪ Display the poster to remember how to use these words correctly in your writing.

Name: _____

Conjunctions: Coordinating

1. Work with a small group to write several sentences about something you would describe as "slime" or "goop." Follow the steps listed below.

   ▪ Brainstorm ideas for a particular topic. Your teacher may help you. ⚠

   ▪ Research as needed to learn about your topic. Your teacher may supply resources. ⚠

   ▪ Take notes and group your information to write sentences.

   ▪ Use coordinating conjunctions in your sentences. Think about which words and phrases are closely related. How can you use coordinating conjunctions to make connections between these ideas?

   _____

   _____

   _____

   _____

   _____

   _____

2. Trade papers with another small group. Use the following tips to mark your classmates' sentences to understand how they used coordinating conjunctions.

   ▪ Draw a box around any coordinating conjunctions.

   ▪ Underline equal words, phrases, or independent clauses that are joined with a coordinating conjunction.

   ▪ Circle any commas used before a coordinating conjunction.

   Example: Hagfish produce slime that clogs the gills of predators, and the predator chokes and leaves.

3. Review your markings to decide whether your classmates used coordinating conjunctions correctly in their writing.

Name: _____

Conjunctions: Coordinating

WRITE

1. Research to learn more about a plant or animal that produces slime. Or, recall your experiences observing slime in a natural setting. Your teacher may supply photographs and resources. 📛

2. Scientists observe things in nature. They record what they see. In the boxes below, record the information you read and observed about a plant or animal that produces slime.

What I learned...	What I observed...
Who would be interested in this information...	Why this information is important...

3. Follow the steps below to write an informative paragraph about your topic.

- Use your notes from #2 above.

- Use coordinating conjunctions in your sentences to make your writing interesting.

- Write your paragraph on a separate piece of paper.

REFLECT

Trade paragraphs with a partner. Answer the questions below to write a response to your partner's paragraph. Use a separate piece of paper.

- What did they discover from their research?

- How did they use coordinating conjunctions to connect closely related ideas?

- What made your partner's writing interesting and effective?

Name: _____

Conjunctions: Subordinating

Conjunctions are words that join parts of a sentence. **Subordinating conjunctions** introduce clauses that cannot stand alone. We call these *dependent clauses*. Subordinating conjunctions connect an independent clause and a dependent clause to make a complex sentence. A subordinating conjunction connects the two ideas in the sentence. It will show a time, place, or cause-and-effect relationship. In a complex sentence, the subordinating conjunction helps readers understand which idea in the sentence is most important.

The main subordinating conjunctions are *after, although, as, because, before, if, once, only, since, so, than, that, though, unless, until, when, whenever, where, wherever,* and *while.*

1. With classmates, read the explanation above.

2. Then read the sample sentences below together.

   - When we think of urban farming, we might think of gardens in a backyard or on a rooftop.

   - Some communities have community gardens that people can rent to grow a garden.

   - Climate change affects urban gardens because plants need the right amount of sun and rain to grow.

3. Discuss the sample sentences above together and answer the questions below.

   - Which subordinating conjunctions are used in the sentences?

   - What is the relationship between the words and phrases that are connected by subordinating conjunctions?

   - What do you notice about how commas are used in the sentences?

   - How do subordinating conjunctions help readers understand the sentences?

4. What have you learned about dependent clauses and subordinating conjunctions in sentences? Use the sentences in #2 as a pattern to work with classmates to write sentences about urban farming. Record your sentences on chart paper or a whiteboard.

Name: _____

Conjunctions: Subordinating

1. Work with a small group to learn more about a part of urban farming that interests you. Your teacher may supply resources.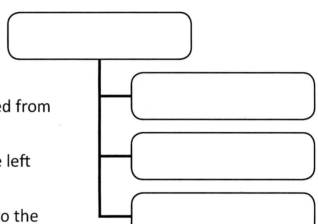

2. On a separate piece of paper, draw a graphic organizer similar to the sample on the right. Follow the steps below to take notes on your graphic organizer.

   ▪ Think about the main ideas you learned from your research.

   ▪ Write the main ideas in the box on the left of your diagram.

   ▪ Write supporting details in the boxes to the right and under each main idea.

3. Use your notes from the graphic organizer to write sentences about your topic. Follow the steps below.

   ▪ Use subordinating conjunctions in your sentences.

   ▪ Write your sentences on a separate piece of paper.

4. Cut apart the clauses in your sentences to make sentence stems. Do not include the subordinating conjunction in the sentence stems.

5. Trade sentence stems with another small group.

6. Follow the tips below to use the clauses your classmates wrote to write new sentences.

   ▪ You may rearrange the clauses in a different way from how they were originally written.

   ▪ Include a subordinating conjunction in each sentence.

   ▪ Think about which clauses are most important, or are the main ideas.

   ▪ Check with your classmates if you need help putting their sentences back together.

Name: _____

Conjunctions: Subordinating

WRITE

1. Your teacher will show you photographs of urban farming, such as rooftop gardens, hydroponics, community gardens, and "green walls." Look at them carefully.

2. Which type of urban farming would you most like to try? Why?

    _____

    _____

3. What are the benefits of urban farming?

    _____

    _____

4. What problems might people face in urban farming?

    _____

    _____

5. Using your notes above, write an opinion paragraph about urban farming. Use a separate piece of paper.

REFLECT

1. Work with a partner to review your opinion paragraphs.

2. How could you use subordinating conjunctions in your sentences to show which ideas are most important?

3. Help each other rewrite at least two sentences from your paragraph to form complex sentences using subordinating conjunctions.

4. Use the following questions to check your new sentences.
    - Are your new sentences clear and easy to understand?
    - Do the new sentences have independent (main) and dependent clauses?
    - Does a subordinating conjunction connect the ideas in each sentence?
    - Does the subordinating conjunction show a time, place, or cause-and-effect relationship in each sentence?
    - Does the subordinating conjunction help readers know which idea in each sentence is most important?

Name: _____

Sentences: Simple

A **simple sentence** has one independent clause, or one complete thought. There are two parts: a *subject* and a *predicate*. The subject tells who or what the sentence is about. Every subject has a noun or pronoun. A simple sentence may have a compound subject, made up of two or more nouns or pronouns and any words that describe the nouns or pronouns. The predicate tells what the subject does in the sentence. Every predicate has a verb. A simple sentence may have a compound predicate, made up of two or more verbs and any words that tell about the action in the sentence.

1. Read the sample sentences below with classmates. For now, ignore the lines below each sentence.

   (a) Gabe jumped on a trampoline on his birthday.

   subject: _____   predicate: _____

   (b) Hannah and Hayley invited Avery to their birthday party.

   subject: _____   predicate: _____

   (c) Every year, Jayden marks his height on a growth chart.

   subject: _____   predicate: _____

   (d) The children drew pictures and signed their names on a birthday card for their teacher.

   subject: _____   predicate: _____

2. On the line below each sentence, write what you notice about the sentence. Is the subject simple or compound? Is the predicate simple or compound?

3. Answer the questions below as you talk about the sentences in #1 with classmates.

   ▪ Which words tell about the verb(s) in the sentences?

   ▪ What do you notice about the word order in each sentence?

4. Work with a small group to write the letter of each sentence on a separate slip of paper.

5. With your group, take turns drawing a slip of paper. State the type of subject and predicate in the sentence for your slip of paper. Say and write a new sentence that follows the same pattern as your example sentence. Write your sentences on a separate piece of paper.

PRACTICE

Name: _____

Sentences: Simple

1. Work with a small group to write questions about how people celebrate birthdays.

_____

_____

_____

_____

2. Trade questions with another small group. Follow the tips below to write simple sentences that answer your classmates' questions.

  - Your answers may answer the questions directly.
  - Your answers may be personal answers based on your experiences.
  - Your answers may be make-believe.
  - Your answers should include a combination of simple and compound subjects and predicates.

_____

_____

_____

_____

3. Take turns sharing your sentences with the classmates who wrote the questions you answered.

4. Talk with your small group about how and why we use simple sentences in our writing. Discuss how your sentences are examples of the points below.

  - We can use simple sentences to communicate ideas clearly.
  - We can use simple sentences to make important points about a topic.
  - We can use simple sentences to summarize a topic.
  - We can use simple sentences to add variety when there are several longer sentences in our writing.

Name: _____

Sentences: Simple

WRITE

1. Read the quotations below.

"A birthday is just the first day of another 365-day journey around the sun. Enjoy the trip!" – Unknown

"There are three hundred and sixty-four days when you might get un-birthday presents, and only one for birthday presents, you know." – Lewis Carroll

2. Answer the questions below to write about one of the quotations in #1.

▪ Do you agree or disagree with the quotation? Why?

_____

_____

▪ What does the quotation mean to you?

_____

_____

_____

▪ How would you compare what the writer says to an experience from your own life?

_____

_____

_____

REFLECT

1. Trade papers with a partner. Write your thoughts about your partner's answers to the questions. Use a separate piece of paper.

2. Talk with your partner about the questions below.

▪ How did you use simple sentences in your writing?

▪ What ideas did you communicate with simple sentences?

▪ What important points did you make with simple sentences?

Name: _____

Sentences: Compound

A **compound sentence** combines two simple sentences (independent clauses) using a comma and a coordinating conjunction. The main coordinating conjunctions are *for, and, nor, but, or, yet,* and *so* (also known as FANBOYS).

We use compound sentences to show the close relationship between two ideas. Often, this relationship shows cause and effect. We use compound sentences to add different sentence lengths to our writing. This makes our writing more natural and interesting.

Examples:
- The woodcutter's youngest son was very little, and he was called Little Tom Thumb.
- The woodcutter's seven children were a burden, for none of them could earn their own living.
- She was poor, but she was their mother.
- He went back to bed, but he did not sleep a wink the rest of the night, thinking what he should do.
- They knocked on the door, and a kind woman opened it.

1. Work with classmates to gather sentences from well-known fairy tales. Your teacher may supply resources. Write the sentences on chart paper or a whiteboard. ⚠

2. Use what you know about simple and compound sentences to divide the sentences into categories. If you find a sentence that does not fit the pattern for a simple or a compound sentence, write it separately.

3. Study the compound sentences you gathered and write your answers to the questions below.

   ▪ What would the fairy tale be like if you rewrote all of the compound sentences as simple sentences?

   _____

   ▪ What do the compound sentences add to the fairy tale?

   _____

   ▪ Which compound sentences show a cause-and-effect relationship?

   _____

4. Talk about your answers to the questions in #3 above with classmates.

PRACTICE

Name: _____

Sentences: Compound

1. Work with a small group to review the examples of compound sentences from the Learn activities on the previous page. Think about how the example compound sentences showed cause-and-effect relationships and made the fairy tale more interesting to read.

2. Use the questions below to brainstorm ideas for your fairy tale. Then complete the story map below.
   - Who are the main characters?
   - Who are the characters who oppose the main characters?
   - What problem do the main characters face?
   - How will the main characters overcome or solve the problem?
   - What events in your story cause something else to happen (cause and effect)?
   - What make-believe or silly things will be in your story?

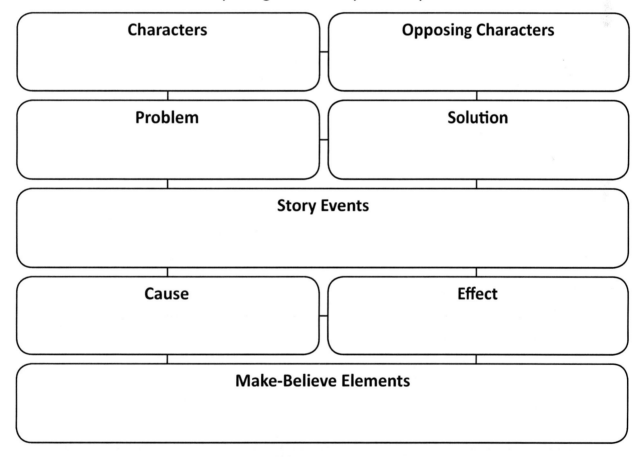

3. Work together to write your fairy tale on separate pieces of paper. Each classmate will need their own copy. Use different types of sentences in your writing, including simple sentences and compound sentences.

4. Share your fairy tale with the class.

Name: _____

Sentences: Compound

WRITE

1. Reread a copy of the fairy tale your small group wrote for the Practice activity.

2. Answer the questions below to think about how you would change the fairy tale. Write your answers as simple sentences.

- What ideas would you add to the fairy tale?

  _____

  _____

- What would happen if you changed the outcome of one of the events in the fairy tale?

  _____

  _____

- What might happen next in the story if the fairy tale continued?

  _____

  _____

3. Combine your ideas from the questions in #2 above. Write compound sentences to add to the fairy tale. Add your sentences in places in the story where they will make the most sense.

REFLECT

Work with a partner who worked in a different small group during the Practice activity. Work together to review the fairy tales your small groups wrote. Write a checkmark next to any statements below that are true of your fairy tales.

- ☐ The writing uses simple sentences correctly.
- ☐ The writing includes compound sentences that are used correctly.
- ☐ Any compound sentences combine two complete ideas (two independent clauses).
- ☐ Any compound sentences connect two simple sentences (independent clauses) with a comma and a coordinating conjunction.
- ☐ The ideas in each compound sentence are related in some way.
- ☐ The compound sentences may show a cause-and-effect event.

Name: _____

Sentences: Complex

A **complex sentence** has an independent clause and a dependent clause.

An *independent clause* is a complete sentence.

Example: Chad uses a computer at school.

A *dependent clause* is not a complete sentence. A subordinating conjunction often starts a dependent clause. The main subordinating conjunctions are *after, although, as, because, before, if, once, only, since, so, than, that, though, unless, until, when, whenever, where, wherever,* and *while.*

Example: when he takes a reading test

A complex sentence has <u>both</u> an independent clause and a dependent clause.

Example: Chad uses a computer at school when he takes a reading test.

When a sentence starts with a dependent clause, a comma is used to set it apart from the independent clause.

Example: Even though Chad checked his computer for a virus, some of the programs still don't work correctly.

A comma is not needed if the dependent clause comes <u>after</u> the independent clause.

Example: Pedro saved the file and printed it after he finished his homework.

We use complex sentences to add meaning and interest to our writing. We use complex sentences to combine short, choppy sentences into longer sentences. Complex sentences show the following relationships between ideas:

- One idea may be stronger than the other idea.
- A complex sentence may show cause and effect.
- A complex sentence may compare or contrast two ideas.
- A complex sentence may show a time relationship.

1. Write a sample sentence about technology for each bulleted item above. Use a separate piece of paper.

2. Write "Yes!" on a slip of paper or cardstock. On the other side, write "Try again!"

3. Take turns sharing the sentences you wrote for #1 with the class.

4. As your classmates share their sentences, hold up the appropriate card. Hold up the "Yes!" card if the sentence is a complex sentence. Hold up the "Try again!" card if the sentence is not a complex sentence.

PRACTICE

Name: _____

Sentences: Complex

1. Work with a small group to brainstorm what you think about cell phones. Write your ideas in the box below.

   ```
   ┌─────────────────────────────────────────────────────────┐
   │                                                           │
   │                                                           │
   │                                                           │
   │                                                           │
   │                                                           │
   └─────────────────────────────────────────────────────────┘
   ```

2. Work together to make connections between ideas. Draw arrows and use different-colored pencils or crayons to show the following types of relationships:
   - Main ideas
   - Supporting ideas
   - Cause and effect (events that happen as a result of something else)
   - Ideas that are similar
   - Ideas that are different
   - Time relationship, such as events that happen before or after other events

3. Use your notes from the activities in #1 and #2 to write complex sentences about cell phones. Write your sentences as a group.

   _____

   _____

   _____

   _____

   _____

   _____

4. As a group, complete the sentence frames below.

   Our sentences are complex sentences because _____

   _____.

   I learned that complex sentences _____

   _____.

YOUR TURN

Name: _____

Sentences: Complex

WRITE

Answer the prompts below to write complex sentences about social media.

▪ How would you explain social media to someone who has not heard that term before?

_____

_____

_____

▪ What do you find most interesting about social media?

_____

_____

▪ How does social media make a difference in people's lives?

_____

_____

_____

▪ How might your life change because of social media?

_____

_____

REFLECT

Use the prompts below to comment on the sentences a classmate wrote in the Write activity above. Write your comments on a separate piece of paper.

▪ Do the complex sentences make sense?

▪ Does each complex sentence have more than one idea?

▪ Does each complex sentence have an independent clause and a dependent clause?

▪ Does each complex sentence have a subordinating conjunction to show how the ideas in the sentence are connected?

Name: _____

Run-on Sentences and Sentence Fragments

A **run-on sentence** combines more than one complete thought or idea. Two or more complete sentences may be put together without any punctuation or connecting word, such as a conjunction.

Example: Astronauts go into space they might spend time on the space station doing experiments.

This is a run-on sentence. It has more than one complete sentence. We can rewrite this run-on sentence as two separate sentences. The rewritten sentences have ending punctuation. They are easier to read and understand.

Example: Astronauts go into space. They might spend time on the space station doing experiments.

A **sentence fragment** is part of a sentence. A sentence fragment <u>does not</u> express a complete thought or idea. A sentence fragment might have a subject or a predicate but not both, or it may have wording that does not make sense.

Example: The astronauts

"The astronauts" is the subject of the sentence. But what is the predicate? What did the astronauts do? The sentence does not tell what the astronauts did. The sentence does not have a predicate. "The astronauts" is a sentence fragment.

1. Write your own definition of a run-on sentence. _____

   _____

2. Write your own definition of a sentence fragment. _____

   _____

3. How can you revise run-on sentences and sentence fragments? _____

   _____

   _____

4. Share your answers to the questions above with classmates. Talk about your ideas for improving and strengthening writing by revising sentences.

PRACTICE

Name: _____

Run-on Sentences and Sentence Fragments

1. Follow the directions below to compete with classmates to identify run-on sentences and sentence fragments in a paragraph.

- Wait for a signal from your teacher to begin reading. 🔲

- Use a colored pencil or crayon to highlight run-on sentences.

- Use a different-colored pencil or crayon to highlight sentence fragments.

2. At the signal, read the paragraph below. Use the colored pencils or crayons you set aside in #1 to highlight run-on sentences and sentence fragments. How many can you find? Set your pencils down when you finish to show you are done.

Machines and equipment can break in space there is not always room to bring more parts and tools to fix things astronauts need to find solutions to such problems. One way to fix a machine. They might use a 3D printer to create parts for a certain mission. Astronauts. Still need to understand. 3D printing works when. An experiment on board the space station is studying small bits of material that can come together like building blocks to make certain things scientists use the bits of material to make other things to meet their needs.

3. Your teacher will group you with classmates who finished close to the same time you finished. Share your answers with your group. Take turns explaining why you highlighted each sentence. 🔲

4. Which of the following tips would be helpful for revising the run-on sentences or sentence fragments you highlighted? Check all that apply.

- ☐ Find subjects and verbs within the long sentence that can go together to make a complete sentence.

- ☐ Look for places where a subordinating conjunction might make the sentence easier to read and understand.

- ☐ Remember to use capital letters and correct ending punctuation in your new sentences.

- ☐ Connect a sentence fragment to a nearby, related complete sentence.

- ☐ Revise a sentence fragment by adding the missing subject or verb to make a complete thought.

5. Work together to rewrite the sentences you highlighted in #2 above. Use a separate piece of paper.

YOUR TURN

Name: _____

Run-on Sentences and Sentence Fragments

WRITE

1. Research to learn and write about a part of space exploration that interests you. Your teacher may supply resources. !

2. Take notes in the box below.

```



```

3. Draw arrows and circles to group the ideas in your notes.

4. Follow the steps below to write an informative paragraph about your topic. Use a separate piece of paper.

- Introduce your topic.
- Develop your topic with facts, definitions, and details.
- Group related information together in a way that makes sense.
- Use linking words to connect ideas.
- Write a concluding sentence.
- If your teacher asks you to, list your sources at the end of your writing. !

REFLECT

1. Trade paragraphs with a partner.

2. Use the tips below to check your partner's writing for run-on sentences.
- Review what you have learned about run-on sentences in this lesson.
- Check for sentences that are hard to understand.
- Check for sentences that have many complete ideas in one sentence.
- Check for complete sentences that are put together without correct punctuation.

3. Use the tips below to check your partner's writing for sentence fragments.
- Review what you have learned about sentence fragments in this lesson.
- Check for sentences that are missing a subject or a predicate.
- Check for sentences that do not express a complete thought.

4. Take turns talking about your review of one another's writing.

Name: _____

Capitalization: Titles

> **Titles** are the names of movies, books, songs, poems, and plays—among other things. All of the important words in a title are capitalized. Articles (*a, an, the*), prepositions (such as *to* and *of*), and coordinating conjunctions (FANBOYS) are not capitalized unless they are the first word in the title. The title is also underlined or italicized for movies, books, and plays. The titles for songs and poems are set apart by quotation marks.
>
> Examples: Movie title: <u>Charlotte's Web</u> or *Charlotte's Web*
> Book title: <u>Stuart Little</u> or *Stuart Little*
> Song title: "Itsy Bitsy Spider"

1. Underline the letter(s) in each title below that you would capitalize.

   - the jungle book
   - homeward bound
   - three blind mice
   - call of the wild
   - because of winn-dixie
   - mary had a little lamb
   - the little red hen
   - doctor dolittle

2. Answer the questions below.

   - What is your favorite book? _____
   - What is your favorite movie? _____
   - What is your favorite song? _____

3. Interview a classmate. Complete the sentence frames below with your classmate's name and their favorite titles.

   - _____'s favorite book is _____
     _____.
   - _____'s favorite movie is _____
     _____.
   - _____'s favorite song is _____
     _____.

4. Share your classmate's favorite titles with the class.

PRACTICE

Name: _____

Capitalization: Titles

1. Work together with a small group to read two poems about animals. Your teacher may give you the poems.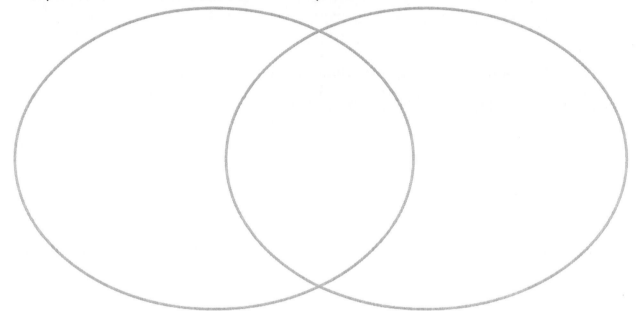

2. Work together to complete a Venn diagram to compare the poems you read. Write the title of each poem over a different part of the diagram. Use correct capitalization and punctuation to write the titles of the poems.

3. Think about the questions below to compare the poems as you complete the Venn diagram above.

   - What is each poem about?

   - How are the poems similar?

   - How are the poems different?

   - What is the author's message in each poem?

4. Work together to write a summary sentence for each poem. Use correct capitalization and punctuation for the titles in your sentences.

   _____

   _____

   _____

   _____

   _____

YOUR TURN

Name: _____

Capitalization: Titles

WRITE

1. What is your favorite book that has also been made into a movie?

   _____

2. How are the book and movie similar? How are they different?

   _____

   _____

3. What other book does this story remind you of? Why?

   _____

   _____

4. What other movie does this story remind you of? Why?

   _____

   _____

5. Write a journal entry to summarize your answers to the questions above. Write complete sentences in an order that makes sense. Use correct capitalization and punctuation when you write titles in your journal entry. Write your journal entry on a separate piece of paper.

REFLECT

1. Trade journal entries with a partner. Think about how you would answer the questions below to write a response to your partner's journal entry.
   - What other book does your partner's favorite book/movie remind you of?
   - What other movie does your partner's favorite book/movie remind you of?
   - How is your partner's favorite book/movie similar to or different from your favorite book or movie?

2. Follow the steps below to write your response to a partner's journal entry.
   - Use correct capitalization and punctuation when you write titles in your response.
   - Write your response on a separate piece of paper.
   - Share your response with your partner.

Grammar and Writing Skills

L E A R N

Name: _____

Punctuation: Addresses

We use **commas** when we write **addresses**. Use a comma to separate the city from the state.

Example: Federal Building
300 N. Los Angeles Street
Los Angeles, California 90012

Use a comma to write out an address when you write it as part of text. The comma separates the street name from the city and state.

Example: First National Bank of Chicago, 1201 W. Madison Street, Chicago, Illinois 60607

1. Read the addresses below and complete the chart.

Lincoln Home National Historic Site
413 S. 8th St.
Springfield, Illinois 62701

Monticello
931 Thomas Jefferson Pkwy
Charlottesville, VA 22902

City	State

2. Read the addresses below and complete the chart.

White House, 1600 Pennsylvania Avenue NW, Washington, DC 20500

Independence Hall, 520 Chestnut Street, Philadelphia, PA 19106

Street	City	State

3. Talk with classmates about the following questions.
   - What do you notice about the addresses in #1 and #2?
   - How did you find the city and state in the addresses in #1?
   - How did you find the street, city, and state names in the addresses in #2?

Name: _____

Punctuation: Addresses

1. Work with a small group to create a map of your community. Draw your map on a separate piece of paper and follow the steps below.

   ▪ Add famous or important buildings in your community to the map.

   ▪ Add main street names you know to the map.

   ▪ Use resources to add street names near the important buildings you drew.

   ▪ Research to find addresses of buildings you added to your map. Your teacher may help you with this. ⚠

   ▪ Write two addresses for important buildings on your map.

   _____   _____

   _____   _____

   _____   _____

2. Imagine you are planning to visit your community, and follow the directions below.

   ▪ Decide which building you might like to visit.

   ▪ Address the envelope below as if you were writing a letter to ask for information.

   ▪ Include your return address or your school's return address on the envelope. Your teacher will give you this information. ⚠

   ▪ Include correct capitalization and punctuation when you write the addresses.

Name: _____

Punctuation: Addresses

WRITE

1. Create an "address book" for a family member or visitor to your community. Answer the questions below to get started.

- Which places would they find most interesting?

  _____

  _____

- For which places might they need the address (for example, a store, library, post office, bank)?

  _____

  _____

2. Follow the steps below to gather information for your address book.

- Research to learn the addresses of the places you will include in your address book. Your teacher may provide resources.

- Write one address you will include in your address book on the lines below.

- Use correct capitalization and punctuation when you write the address.

Name: _____

Street: _____

City: _____ **State:** _____ **Zip Code:** _____

REFLECT

Answer the reflection questions below on a separate piece of paper.

- Why do we use addresses?

- How do we remember addresses we want to know?

- Why is it important to use capital letters and correct spelling in addresses?

- Why is it important to use correct punctuation in addresses?

Name: _____

Punctuation: Possessives

We can use an **apostrophe** to make a noun **possessive**. A possessive noun shows ownership. We make a word possessive by adding an *'s*.

Example: Rosa Parks refused to obey a bus driver's demand to move to a different seat.

The demand belongs to the bus driver.

We form the possessive of a plural noun ending in *s* by adding just an apostrophe.

Example: The buses' drivers enforced rules for separate seating areas.

The buses have drivers.

When more than one person, place, or thing shares ownership, add *'s* to only the last noun in the series.

Example: The boycott affected Rosa, Samuel, and Thelma's travel plans for over a year.

The travel plans belong to Rosa, Samuel, and Thelma.

Its, without an apostrophe, is possessive.

Example: Its members elected Dr. Martin Luther King, Jr., as their president.

The members belong to "it." We would read the sentences before or after this sentence to understand who or what "it" is.

If *its* has an apostrophe (*it's*), then it becomes the contraction for *it is*.

1. Read the paragraph below.

   Harriet Beecher Stowe had many brothers and sisters. Harriet's seven brothers became ministers. Two of her sisters helped shape Harriet's political views. Harriet's father and husband shared her opinions about slavery. Harriet loved to read. She decided to express her feelings about slavery by writing a book. The first part of Harriet's book was printed in a newspaper in 1851. The next year, her work <u>Uncle Tom's Cabin</u> was published as a book. Many people believe Harriet's writing influenced public opinion before the Civil War.

2. Circle the possessive nouns in the paragraph above.

3. Follow the steps below to create a web about Harriet Beecher Stowe.
   - Work with classmates to draw a simple web on chart paper or a whiteboard.
   - Write the name of the person in the center circle of your web.
   - Look back at the nouns you circled in #2. What people, places, things, or ideas belong to this famous person? Write the nouns that belong to this famous person in other circles on your web.

Name: _____

Punctuation: Possessives

1. Work with a small group to review the web you created with classmates in the Learn activity.

2. What other people, places, things, or ideas might belong to a famous person? Brainstorm with your group and write your ideas in the box below.

   [ ]

3. Work together to research a famous person. Think about people who have contributed something to history or science. Which famous person will you research? Your teacher may help you with this. ✎

   _____

4. What people, places, things, or ideas belong to that person? Take notes in the chart below.

People	Places	Things	Ideas

5. Use your notes to write sentences about your famous person. Include possessives in your sentences.

   _____

   _____

   _____

   _____

Name: _____

Punctuation: Possessives

WRITE

1. Research another famous person of interest to you. Take notes to remember the people, places, things, or ideas that belong to that person. Use a web or a chart, if you wish, to help organize your notes. Your teacher may help you with this. Write your notes on a separate piece of paper. ⚡

2. Use your notes to write a paragraph about the person you researched. Remember to use possessives correctly in your sentences.

_____

_____

_____

_____

_____

_____

REFLECT

1. Trade papers with a partner.

2. In the box below, write the possessives your partner used in their writing. Write each possessive as a phrase (for example, George Washington's horse).

3. What have you learned about using possessives in your writing? Talk with your partner and write your answer below.

_____

_____

Name: _____

Punctuation: Dialogue

> Use **quotation marks** to show what someone said. Write the quotation marks before and after the words the speaker says. The first word within the quotation marks is always capitalized. Punctuation marks, such as commas, are usually placed within the quotation marks.
>
> Example: "Will we watch cartoons this Saturday?" asked Kenneth.
>
> We use a **comma** to set off the exact words of a speaker from the rest of the sentence.
>
> Example: "My favorite cartoon has a pretend tiger in it," said Brian.

1. With classmates, answer the questions below about favorite cartoon characters. Share your answers aloud.
   - What makes different cartoon characters interesting?
   - How does each character act that is different from other characters?
   - How do different cartoon characters talk?

2. Work together to decide on an experience one or more cartoon characters might have (for example, a cartoon character must save others from a natural disaster). List your ideas in the box below.

   [ ]

3. Answer the questions below to talk with classmates about a comic strip you will create together as a class. A comic strip has several boxes, or frames, that tell a story or experience.
   - What events will be part of the experience or story your comic strip will tell?
   - What will the characters say?
   - What actions will the characters do?

4. Follow the steps below to create a comic strip with classmates. Create your comic strip on chart paper or a whiteboard.
   - Take turns drawing each frame.
   - Take turns drawing pictures to show the characters' actions.
   - Take turns writing the dialogue the characters say in speech bubbles or captions.
   - Work together to arrange your frames in an order that makes sense to complete your comic strip.

Name: _____

Punctuation: Dialogue

1. Work with a small group to talk about cartoons you have watched or comic strips you have read. Answer the following questions.

   ▪ What kinds of characters are in the cartoons?

   ▪ What kinds of things happen to these characters?

   ▪ How do the characters respond to what happens? What do they do? What do they say?

2. Work together to think of your own cartoon characters. Talk about how you would answer the questions above for your own characters and a scene or experience from their life. Write your answers on a separate piece of paper.

3. Take turns drawing the characters for your cartoon scene.

4. Follow the steps below to write your cartoon scene as a skit.

   ▪ Look at the drawings you made in #3.

   ▪ Take turns writing what the characters say and do in the scene. Use a separate piece of paper.

   ▪ Write the dialogue with correct punctuation.

5. Decide which group members will play which roles in your skit. Practice your skit, using the dialogue and actions you wrote in #4.

6. Perform your skit for the class.

Punctuation: Dialogue

WRITE

1. Who is your favorite cartoon character? _____

2. Why do you like this character? _____

_____

3. What kinds of things does this character do and say? _____

_____

4. What happens to this character? _____

_____

5. Follow the steps below to imagine yourself in a scene with this character.
  - Write your cartoon or comic strip on a separate piece of paper.
  - Draw yourself and the cartoon character in a scene. Where are you? What does it look like?
  - Draw any other characters who are also in the scene. What do they look like? What are they doing?
  - Write dialogue to go with the scene. Use speech bubbles or captions. What are you and your cartoon character saying?
  - What happened in the scene? What will you do or say in response to what happened?

REFLECT

1. Complete the sentences below.

  - We use _____ to show what someone said.

  - In a story or scene, the words someone says are called _____.

  - The first word in a quotation is always _____.

  - We use a _____ to set off the exact words of a speaker from the rest of the sentence.

2. Check your comic strip. Did you use punctuation correctly in the dialogue you wrote?

3. Revise your writing as needed. When we use punctuation correctly in dialogue, others can easily understand who is speaking and what that person says.

Name: _____

Types of Writing: Opinion

We use different types of writing for different reasons.

Sometimes, we write to state an opinion. An opinion is what we think or believe about something. **Opinion writing** says what we think or feel about a topic. It gives reasons for readers to agree with the opinion. It may ask readers to change their thinking to agree with the stated opinion. It may ask readers to do something.

We all have opinions about family vacations. We might enjoy vacations with our family very much. We might wish we could invite a friend to come with us on a family vacation. We might think our family should go to a certain place for vacation. We have reasons for our opinions.

1. Read the following opinions. On the line before each statement, write "yes" or "no" to show if you agree or disagree with the opinion.

   _____ I love to go to different places.

   _____ I like to travel with someone who likes to do the same things I like.

   _____ I wish I could invite a friend to come on our next family vacation.

   _____ You should always learn something new on a family vacation.

   _____ It's fun to walk to see different things on vacation.

   _____ I would want to try new food, explore a farmer's market, or have a picnic on a family vacation.

2. Review the opinions with classmates. Take turns sharing your response to each opinion and give a reason for your response.

3. Write an opinion statement to express what you think about the question below. Why do families take vacations?

   _____

   _____

4. Write the reason for the opinion statement you wrote in #3.

   _____

   _____

Name: _____

Types of Writing: Opinion

1. Work with a small group to choose one of the opinion statements from Learn #1. What is the group consensus? Do most group members agree or disagree with the opinion? Check the box below that fits your group's opinion.

    ☐ Agree   ☐ Disagree

2. Work together to write an opinion statement that expresses your opinion about the statement you chose in #1 above.

    _____

    _____

3. List reasons for your group's opinion below. Write your reasons in order from most important to least important.

    most _____

    _____

    least _____

4. Draw arrows to show which reasons connect to other reasons on the list. Or, draw arrows to show which reasons connect directly to the opinion statement you wrote in #2.

5. Talk with your group about how your reasons connect to the opinion statement you wrote in #2 above.

6. On a separate piece of paper, write your own opinion paragraph about the opinion statement you wrote with your small group. Follow the tips below to write your paragraph.

    ▪ Introduce the topic of your paragraph by writing your own opinion about the statement you talked about in your small group.

    ▪ Give reasons for your opinion that connect to the statement you wrote at the beginning of your paragraph.

    ▪ Use linking words and phrases you have learned to connect your reasons to your opinion statement.

    ▪ Write a sentence that concludes your paragraph. Convince readers that your opinion is reasonable, suggest that they consider agreeing with your opinion, or ask them to do something different in their own life.

YOUR TURN

Name: _____

Types of Writing: Opinion

WRITE

1. What do you like best about going places with your family?

_____

_____

2. What are your reasons for this opinion?

_____

_____

_____

_____

3. Write an opinion paragraph about what you like best about going places with your family. Use the tips in Practice #6 to help you. Write your paragraph on a separate piece of paper.

4. Draw a picture to illustrate your paragraph. Use the same separate piece of paper.

5. If possible, record yourself reading your opinion paragraph aloud. Present the recording to a family member, along with your drawing, or share it at a classroom open house.

REFLECT

1. Take turns reading your opinion paragraphs aloud to classmates.

2. Write one thing a classmate did well in their opinion paragraph.

_____

_____

3. Write one way that same classmate could connect their reasons to the stated opinion to make the paragraph easier for readers to understand.

_____

_____

4. Share your feedback in #2 and #3 with your classmate.

Name: _____

Types of Writing: Informative

We use different types of writing for different reasons.

Informative writing tells about someone or something. It gives information. This kind of writing has facts and details. A fact is a detail that has been checked and shown to be correct. We also use this kind of writing to tell how to do something or how something works.

This kind of writing answers questions. We can ask *who, what, when, where, why,* and *how* to plan our writing.

Informative writing often groups facts and details in a way that makes sense. We use linking words to connect ideas within these categories of information.

1. Read the following paragraph with classmates.

   Some vehicles ride on a cushion of air. A general word for these vehicles is *hovercraft*. The first hovercraft traveled across the English Channel. They carried people and cars from southern England to northern France. These huge vehicles carried more than 50 cars and over 400 people per trip. They used a lot of fuel and became too expensive to maintain and operate. Now, there are smaller air cushion vehicles (ACVs) around the world. Many are used for sport, coastal ferries, or military purposes.

2. Look back at what you read to answer the questions in the boxes below. Not all questions will have an answer.

Who?	Where?
What?	**Why?**
When?	**How?**

3. Circle any words or phrases you wrote that connect one idea to another idea in the paragraph you read in #1. Talk with classmates about how these words guide readers through the information. What other words could the author use to connect ideas about this topic? Take turns listing your ideas on chart paper or a whiteboard.

Name: _____

Types of Writing: Informative

1. What would be a fun way to travel? Work with a small group to brainstorm a different or unique form of transportation. On the line below, write a form of transportation you would like to know more about.

_____

Use the question words (*who, what, when, where, why,* and *how*) to write questions you might ask about that form of transportation.

_____

_____

_____

_____

_____

_____

2. Work together to research to learn about the form of transportation you noted in #1. Your teacher may supply resources. Take notes and group information into categories for each question word that the facts, details, and examples might answer. Note your sources so that others can check your facts and read more information about the topic if they so choose.

3. Assign each group member a question word. Each group member will use their research notes to write an informative paragraph that answers their question word.

4. Work together as a group to compile your writing, following the steps below.

- Work together to write one or two sentences to introduce your topic.

- Arrange the paragraphs in an order that makes sense.

- Check each paragraph to make sure it develops the topic clearly.

- Work together to add linking words and phrases to connect individual paragraphs and ideas. Look back at the list you wrote with classmates in Learn #3 if you need help.

- Work together to write a concluding statement for your informative piece.

YOUR TURN

Name: _____

Types of Writing: Informative

WRITE

1. Informative writing provides facts, details, and examples about a topic. It answers questions such as *who, what, when, where, why,* and *how.* Write question sentences to ask a classmate about the form of transportation they researched with their small group in the Practice activity.

   _____

   _____

   _____

   _____

   _____

2. Ask your questions of a classmate who worked in a different small group during the Practice activity. Remind your partner to answer the questions with information they learned when they researched their topic and wrote informative paragraphs with their group.

3. Take notes to record your partner's answers to your questions. Use a separate piece of paper.

4. Use your notes to write an article for a class newspaper or magazine about interesting forms of transportation.

5. Work together with classmates to gather your articles into a class newspaper or magazine.

REFLECT

1. Trade papers with a different partner.

2. Use the checklist below to help your partner think about how well their writing communicates information effectively.

   ☐ The paragraph introduces a topic (this might be one part of a larger topic).

   ☐ The paragraph includes facts, details, and other information about the topic.

   ☐ The information is organized in a way that makes sense.

   ☐ The paragraph includes linking words to connect ideas.

   ☐ The paragraph might have a sentence that concludes that part of the information.

Name: _____

Types of Writing: Narrative

We use different types of writing for different reasons.

Sometimes, we write a story. This is called **narrative writing**. We use this type of writing to share experiences. We tell what happened to us or to a character. Narrative writing can be real or make-believe. It tells events that happened in an order that makes sense.

Narrative writing has action. The stories tell about people, places, or things, and how they look, sound, smell, taste, or feel. Often, characters solve a problem. We read this kind of writing to learn about people and their experiences. We read narrative writing for fun.

1. Which stories have you read or watched that have to do with time travel in the past or in the future?

    _____

    _____

    _____

2. Choose one story title. Talk about the questions below with classmates to think about narrative writing in this story.

    - How does the story begin? How does the author introduce the situation and characters?

    - Why is it important for events in a story to happen in a way that makes sense?

    - What do characters in the story say and do to show how they respond to what happens in the story?

    - How does the story end? What makes readers feel satisfied with the way it ends?

3. Where and when would you go in the past, present, or future? What might happen if you traveled to a different time? Write your ideas in the boxes below.

Past	Present	Future

Name: _____

Types of Writing: Narrative

1. Look at the photographs below.

2. With a small group, follow the steps below to gather ideas for a story about one of the photographs.

- Choose one photograph to write about.

- To what other place or time (past, present, or future) might that door lead? Write your ideas on a separate piece of paper.

- Pass your paper to the person on your right.

- Whom or what would you take with you to enter the door your classmate described above? Write your answer on your classmate's piece of paper.

- Pass your paper to the person on your right.

- Whom or what might you meet if you walk through the door your classmate described above? Write your answer on your classmate's piece of paper.

- Pass your paper to the person on your right.

- What might happen once you walk through the door your classmate described above? Write your answer on your classmate's piece of paper.

3. Pass your paper to its owner. Use your classmates' notes to draft a story about traveling back in time or forward to the future. Think about the following questions to plan your story. Write your story on a separate piece of paper.

- How will you introduce the setting and characters to readers?

- What happens in the story?

- How do characters react to what happens?

- How will the story end?

Name: _____

Types of Writing: Narrative

WRITE

1. Review your notes from Learn #3. What ideas from your notes could you use to revise the story you drafted in Practice #3?

2. Review the notes and ideas you received from classmates during the Practice activity. What changes and additions would you make to your story idea in #1 above? Write your ideas in the box below.

```



```

3. Follow the steps below to write a final copy of your story about traveling to a different place or time.

    ▪ Use your notes from Learn #3 and the ideas your classmates wrote in the Practice activity.

    ▪ Write your story on a separate piece of paper.

    ▪ Think about how you would answer each question in Learn #2 for your story.

    ▪ Check your writing to make sure you have developed your story in a way that makes sense and is interesting for readers.

REFLECT

Trade papers with a partner. Read your partner's story and complete the sentence frames below to offer feedback on the story topic. Remember, we each like different kinds of stories because we have our own interests.

▪ I would like to travel in time with you because _____

_____ .

▪ I would travel with you, but I think we should go to _____ because
(place)

_____ .

▪ I would rather stay right here and now because _____

_____ .

Name: _____

Formal and Informal English

> We use **formal English** to write or speak to people who we respect. When we use formal English, we choose more formal words. We use correct spelling and punctuation and write in complete sentences. We use formal English to write a school paper or to give a speech.
>
> We use **informal English** to write or speak to friends or people we know well. We may write numbers or symbols in place of letters. We may use more informal words, including contractions. We do not always write in complete sentences. We use informal English to write a letter, an email, or a text message or when we call a friend.

1. Read the paragraph below.

   Each new fitness program has its own focus. One program was started by a woman. It is called Orangetheory. Each class has a different focus, but they all last for only one hour. The goal of this fitness program is to spend as much time as possible in a higher target heart-rate zone. The idea is that intense workouts lead to better overall fitness.

2. Is the paragraph in #1 written in formal or informal English? Underline words and phrases that help you answer the question.

   _____

3. Read the paragraph below.

   Hey, did u know crossfit has classes for kids? I'm gonna check it out. Everyone says it's really cool and lots of fun. It says here you don't need a lotta equipment & even some schools use it.

4. Is the paragraph in #3 written in formal or informal English? Underline words and phrases that help you answer the question.

   _____

5. Who do you know that might like to read the first paragraph? Why?

   _____

6. Who do you know that might like to read the second paragraph? Why?

   _____

7. Discuss your answers to the questions above with classmates. Talk about the differences between formal and informal English. Work together to create a checklist you could use to make sure your writing has the features of formal English. Write your checklist on chart paper or a whiteboard.

PRACTICE

Name: _____

Formal and Informal English

1. What fitness or exercise trends have you heard or read about?

   _____

   _____

   _____

2. Write a sentence using formal English to describe one kind of exercise you know about.

   _____

   _____

   _____

3. Write a sentence using informal English to say something about one kind of exercise you know about.

   _____

   _____

   _____

4. Follow the directions below to play a beanbag toss game with a small group.

   ▪ The first player will say something in formal English about a fitness trend or an exercise they have heard or read about. That person will then toss a beanbag or another soft object to another person in the group.

   ▪ The second player will use informal English to respond to the first player's statement.

   ▪ The next player may use formal English to respond to what has already been said. Or, they may make a new statement about fitness and exercise.

   ▪ Continue with players taking turns using formal and informal English to make and respond to statements about fitness and exercise.

5. Talk with your group about the questions below.

   ▪ What did you notice about using formal and informal English?

   ▪ What did you learn about using formal English to speak?

   ▪ How will understanding these differences help you speak and listen in the classroom or other learning environments?

Name: _____

Formal and Informal English

WRITE

1. Which fitness trend or form of exercise most interests you?

   _____

2. Research as needed to gather information about the topic you wrote in #1 above. Your teacher may supply resources. Note facts, details, and examples about your topic, as well as your sources. Use a separate piece of paper. ✏️

3. Write a letter to a friend or family member to tell them about your topic. Use informal English. Write your letter on a separate piece of paper.

4. Why might informal English be the best way to communicate your ideas in #3 above?

   _____

   _____

   _____

   _____

REFLECT

1. Work with a partner to choose a fitness trend or form of exercise you would like to see offered in your school or community.

2. Follow the tips below to write a letter to someone in your school or community to request that they offer this exercise or fitness class to children your age.

   - Use your notes from the Practice and Write activities for ideas. Do additional research if needed.

   - Review what you have learned about opinion writing. Remember, with opinion writing, you want to convince readers to agree with your stated opinion and possibly take action.

   - Work with your partner to compose a letter using formal English.

   - If possible, address and mail your letter to the actual person you want to receive the letter.

3. Talk with your partner about the differences you noticed in writing an informal letter to a friend or family member and writing a formal letter to someone you do not know well. How will understanding these differences help you in other learning activities?

Name: _____

Vocabulary: Synonyms and Antonyms

A **synonym** is one word that has a similar meaning to another word. *House* and *dwelling* are synonyms. *House* and *dwelling* both mean a place where people live.

Antonyms are two words with opposite meanings. *Large* and *small* are antonyms. *Large* and *small* have opposite meanings. *Large* means that something is great in size or amount. *Small* means that something is little or not great in size or amount.

When we write, we want others to understand what we want to say. We use synonyms and antonyms to help us choose just the right word.

1. *Dwelling* is a synonym for *house*. What other synonyms for *house* do you know? Or, what other types of housing can you list?

   _____   _____

   _____   _____

2. What words do we use to describe different types of houses? Some of these words might be synonyms of each other. List your words in the left column below.

   _____   _____

   _____   _____

   _____   _____

3. What antonyms that have opposite meanings from the words you listed in #2 above can we use to describe houses? Write those words in the right column above.

4. Follow the directions below to play a game with classmates.
   ▪ Form two teams: "Synonyms" and "Antonyms."
   ▪ Your teacher will call out a word related to houses. 🔔
   ▪ Teams will take turns: the Synonym team will try to say a synonym for the word, and the Antonym team will try to say an antonym for the word.
   ▪ You and your teammates may use your word lists from #1, #2, and #3 above for ideas.
   ▪ Teams receive one point each time they are able to say a synonym or an antonym correctly.

Name: _____

Vocabulary: Synonyms and Antonyms

1. Look at the photographs below. Write words to describe each dwelling on the lines below the pictures.

_____   _____

_____   _____

_____   _____

_____   _____

2. Share your words with a small group. Which words did your classmates write that are synonyms of your words? Add them to the words you wrote.

3. Talk with others in your group about antonyms for your words. When or why might you want to use antonyms? Write ideas shared in your group on a separate piece of paper.

4. Work together to write a story about one of the photographs. Use a separate piece of paper. Think about the questions below to get started.
   ▪ Who might live in this type of dwelling?
   ▪ What interesting qualities would you give the character(s)?
   ▪ What problem(s) might the main character face?
   ▪ What will happen in the story?
   ▪ How will the character(s) resolve the problem(s)?
   ▪ How is this house important to the story? What role will the dwelling play in the story?

5. Share your story with other classmates.

Name: _____

Vocabulary: Synonyms and Antonyms

WRITE

1. In what kind of house would you like to live?

   _____

2. Draw a picture of the house. Use a separate piece of paper.

3. Write sentences to describe this house. Use synonyms and antonyms in your sentences to describe the house for someone who will not see your picture.

   _____

   _____

   _____

   _____

   _____

   _____

4. Turn over your drawing.

REFLECT

1. Trade papers with a classmate. Read your partner's sentences.

2. Turn over the papers with your partner's sentences and drawing. Use a separate piece of paper to draw what you think the house they described looks like.

3. Turn over your partner's drawing and compare it to the picture you just drew. How well were you able to picture your partner's house using their description?

   _____

   _____

   _____

4. Talk with your partner about how using synonyms and antonyms in our writing helps us describe exactly what we want to say. How does this help readers form a mental picture? Share your ideas with the class.

Name: _____

Vocabulary: Words and Phrases for Effect

When we write, we want readers to understand what we're trying to say. We want to use words that say exactly what we mean. We use words to give readers a mental picture. A *thesaurus* is a book that lists synonyms and antonyms for words. We can use a thesaurus to find a stronger, more precise, or more descriptive word.

We can use words and phrases to make a story or scene sound exciting, dangerous, or silly. Descriptive words help readers imagine the mood of a story, or what the characters are like. Precise verbs help us picture the action in a scene or story.

Study the example below to learn more about using **words and phrases for effect**.

Example: One day, Sam's mother and father agreed he needed new clothes. His mother made him a dazzling red coat and a pair of blue pants. Sam's father went to the bazaar and bought him a stunning green umbrella and a pair of purple shoes with crimson soles. Sam put on all his fine clothes. As he walked through the jungle, he met a tiger. Sam bargained with the tiger, and they agreed Sam would not be harmed in exchange for his dazzling red coat. Upon meeting a second tiger, Sam had to make another deal to save his life. This tiger made Sam give him the blue pants. By this time, Sam had only his stunning green umbrella to cover himself and his purple shoes with crimson soles.

(adapted from *Little Black Sambo* by Helen Bannerman)

1. Look at the photographs below.

2. On a separate piece of paper, write words to describe each picture. Try to include sensory details for each scene.

3. Take turns with classmates sharing the words you wrote to describe each photograph. Answer the questions below as you talk about the pictures.
   - What do you notice about each scene?
   - What effect does each picture have on you? How does it make you feel?
   - What words did you use to describe the photograph's effect? Why did you choose these particular words?

PRACTICE

Name: _____

Vocabulary: Words and Phrases for Effect

1. Read the excerpt below with a small group.

"I will call Mowgli and he shall say the Master Words—if he will," said Baloo, the serious, old brown bear.

"My head is buzzing like a bee-tree," said a sullen voice over their heads. Mowgli slid down a tree trunk, very angry. "I come for Bagheera and not for you, fat, old Baloo!"

"That is all the same to me," said Baloo, hurt and grieved.

"Master Words for which people?" said Mowgli, delighted to show off. "The jungle has many tongues. I know them all!"

After he had said them all, Mowgli kicked up his feet behind and clapped his hands together to applaud himself. Then he jumped on Bagheera's back and sat sideways, drumming with his heels on the panther's glossy skin. Then he made the worst faces he could think of at Baloo. "There, there! That was worth a little bruise," said the Brown Bear, tenderly.

(adapted from *The Jungle Book* by Rudyard Kipling)

2. Answer the questions below independently to think about the story.

   ▪ What happens in this scene? _____

   _____

   ▪ How did the characters respond to what happened? _____

   _____

   _____

   ▪ How did the scene make you feel? _____

   _____

3. Share your answers to the questions above with your small group.

4. Talk about words and phrases the author used for effect. Highlight them with colored pencils, crayons, or markers.

5. Talk about the questions below to think about how the author used words and phrases for effect.

   ▪ What do you notice about these words and phrases?
   ▪ How do you think the author wanted readers to think or feel?

Name: _____

Vocabulary: Words and Phrases for Effect

WRITE

1. Follow the steps below to imagine you are in a jungle.

   ▪ Draw a line across the bottom third of a separate piece of paper.

   ▪ Gather green pencils, pens, and markers. Use the different colors of green to lightly shade the area above the line you drew on your paper.

   ▪ Use a black pencil, pen, or marker to draw a figure representing yourself in the middle of the green "jungle."

2. Close your eyes and imagine what is around you in the jungle. Open your eyes and think about how you would answer the questions below.

   ▪ What do you see and hear?

   ▪ What does it smell like?

   ▪ What can you reach out and touch?

   ▪ What would you feel if you were barefoot?

   ▪ How do you feel?

3. Draw what you imagined is around you in the jungle.

4. In the space below the line on your paper, write words and phrases to describe how you would answer the questions in #2 above. Use a thesaurus for ideas.

5. Write a descriptive paragraph or story about your imaginary experience in the jungle. Include the words and phrases you wrote for #4. Use a separate piece of paper to write your story.

REFLECT

1. Trade paragraphs with a partner and read your partner's writing.

2. Highlight words and phrases your partner used for effect.

3. Follow the steps below to imagine you are in the scene with your partner.

   ▪ Draw a web on a separate piece of paper. Include five circles in the web.

   ▪ Label each circle with one of the five senses.

   ▪ Review the words you highlighted in your partner's writing. How do they make you feel?

   ▪ Describe what you would experience in the scene with each sense.

Vocabulary: Root Words and Prefixes

Name: _____

A **root word** is a base word without a prefix added to it. It is the smallest part of the word that has meaning.

A **prefix** is added to the beginning of a root word. A prefix changes the meaning of the word. We learn common prefixes and their meanings to help us figure out the meanings of new words.

Examples:

dis + root word = **not or opposite**   **in** + root word = **not**

dis + like = not liking   *in* + active = not active

1. Read the sample sentences below with classmates.
   - Dinosaurs were <u>unbelievably</u> large animals that roamed the planet many years ago.
   - We were not alive during the time of the dinosaurs, so their world is rather <u>indescribable</u> to us.
   - A dinosaur flying through the air seems <u>unreal</u> to imagine.
   - Some of the dinosaurs were very <u>unusual</u> creatures.
   - Some people are in complete <u>disbelief</u> that dinosaurs ever lived.
   - I wonder if we will ever find that some of our ideas about dinosaurs are <u>incorrect</u>.
   - Wouldn't it be something if dinosaurs were to <u>reappear</u>!
   - Some scientists think dinosaurs would be <u>unable</u> to survive in our current climate.

2. Take turns describing how you could figure out the meaning of the underlined words. Use the tips below to help you.
   - What is the root word of each new word?
   - How can you figure out the meaning of the root word?
   - What is the prefix attached to the root word?
   - What is the meaning of the prefix?
   - What is the meaning of the whole new word?

3. Work with classmates to write your own sentences using the new prefixes you have learned. Write your sentences on chart paper or a whiteboard. Your sentences may be about dinosaurs, other reptiles, fossils, or different climates.

Name: _____

Vocabulary: Root Words and Prefixes

1. Follow the steps below and work with a small group to learn more about prefixes.

   ▪ Study the prefix examples presented in the Learn activity.

   ▪ Review prefixes you may have already learned, such as *un-* and *re-*.

   ▪ Use a dictionary or other resources to become familiar with words that include these prefixes.

   ▪ List new words with prefixes you have learned. Write your words in the correct boxes below.

dis-	in-	re-	un-

2. What other words with prefixes did you find in your word study? Use the tips below for ideas.

   ▪ Think about root words that have a different meaning with a prefix added.

   ▪ Talk with others in your group about words they know that use prefixes.

   ▪ Think about words we use to talk or write about dinosaurs or related topics.

   ▪ On a separate piece of paper, draw blank boxes. Label the blank boxes with any prefixes that are different from those listed in #1. Write words with that prefix in the box.

3. Talk with your small group about the meanings of the words you listed in #1 and #2 above. Use a dictionary or other resources to check the meanings.

4. Write a sentence using one new word you learned.

   _____

   _____

5. Share the sentence you wrote in #4 with a classmate, friend, or family member.

YOUR TURN

Name: _____

Vocabulary: Root Words and Prefixes

WRITE

1. What topic or idea about dinosaurs interests you?

_____

_____

2. Plan an article about dinosaurs. Use the tips below to help you. Then write your article on a separate piece of paper.

- Your article may express an opinion, give facts and other information about dinosaurs, or present both sides of an issue related to dinosaurs.
- Try to use prefixes in your writing.
- Use your word lists from the Practice activity and the prefixes and words you learned in the Learn activity.

_____

_____

_____

_____

_____

_____

_____

_____

REFLECT

1. Trade articles with a partner and read their writing.

2. Underline any words in your classmate's writing that have prefixes.

3. Check to see if they used the words correctly in each sentence. Does the meaning of each word you underlined make sense in its sentence?

4. Work together to write the meaning of each word you underlined in your partner's writing. Write the words and their meanings on a separate piece of paper. Draw a star by any word that is new to you.

Name: _____

Vocabulary: Root Words and Suffixes

A **suffix** is added to the end of the root word. Some suffixes change the meaning or the tense of the word. Often, suffixes change the part of speech of the word. Sometimes, we change the spelling of the root word when we add a suffix.

Examples:

root word + *ful* = full of

pain + *ful* = full of pain

root word + *less* = without

fear + *less* = without fear

root word + *y* = full of, somewhat like

dream + *y* = like a dream

root word + *ly* = characteristic of

soft + *ly* = having the characteristic of being soft

1. Read the example sentences below.

   ▪ Kiarra was restless while she waited for the robot to finish its job.

   ▪ A robot that cleans would be a delightful thing to have.

   ▪ Robots can be useful in our everyday lives.

   ▪ Some robots dress people, and they do it gently.

   ▪ Some robots do things for people who are helpless because they are sick or hurt.

   ▪ The robot helped Avett clean the messy room.

2. Underline the word with a suffix in each sentence.

3. Talk with classmates about how the suffix changes the meaning of each word.

4. How many words can you think of using the suffixes you learned above? Follow the directions below to challenge yourself with classmates.

   ▪ Write one word with each suffix to get started.

   _____   _____

   _____   _____

   _____   _____

   _____   _____

   ▪ Take turns saying a word that has a suffix.

5. What are some words you heard your classmates say? Add them to the lines above.

Name: _____

Vocabulary: Root Words and Suffixes

1. Work together with a small group to make a game for classmates. Think about the questions below to create your game.

- What word games do you already know how to play?

- How will players use root words and suffixes in your game?

- Will your game have a game board?

- Will your game have word cards?

- What will players do when it's their turn?

- How will the game start? How will it end?

2. Take notes about your ideas as you talk with others in your group about the questions above.

3. Use paper, cardstock, or poster board and colored pencils or crayons to make your game. Write neatly.

4. Work together to write directions to tell how to play your game. Use a separate piece of paper.

5. Trade games with another small group. Follow the game directions your classmates wrote and play their game.

Name: _____

Vocabulary: Root Words and Suffixes

WRITE

1. Answer the questions below to think about how robots interest you. If you need ideas, research and take notes. Your teacher may supply resources. ▮

▪ How can robots help people?

_____

_____

▪ How might robots learn how to do different tasks?

_____

_____

▪ How do you think robots will be used in the near future?

_____

_____

2. Write an opinion or informative paragraph about robots. Include suffixes in your writing to say exactly what you want to say without using extra words. Use a separate piece of paper to write your paragraph.

REFLECT

1. Trade papers with a partner and answer the questions below about your partner's paragraph. Write your comments on a separate piece of paper.
   ▪ Which suffixes did your partner use in their writing?
   ▪ How did each suffix change the meaning of the root word?
   ▪ How does the meaning of this new word add to the meaning of the sentence?
   ▪ How did your partner use suffixes to describe people, things, or actions?

2. Talk with your partner about the comments you wrote in #1.

3. Review how suffixes change the meaning of root words.

4. Talk with your partner about how we can use suffixes to make new words as people make and do new things in our changing world.

5. Share your ideas with classmates.

Name: _____

Vocabulary: Context Clues

We learn new words in different ways. We use these new words when we read, write, and speak. One way we learn new words is through reading. Sometimes, we do not know what a word means. We can look at the words in the sentence before and after the new word. These **context clues** can help us learn what a new word means.

1. Read the tips below with classmates to learn how to find context clues in sentences.
    - Read the words before and after the new word.
    - Read the sentences before and after the sentence with the new word.
    - Look for clues to figure out the part of speech of the new word.
    - Look for words that might have the same or opposite meaning as the new word (synonyms or antonyms).
    - Look for words grouped with the new word to find clues for the new word's meaning.

2. Read the sample sentences below. Talk with classmates about the examples of context clues in the sentences that help readers understand the underlined word.

    Many different plants and animals live together in the ocean <u>biome</u>. There are living and nonliving things in this environment. The climate can be very cold or it can be warm.

3. Turn and talk with a classmate about ways we use this language skill. Take notes to answer the questions below.

    - How do we use context clues when we read?

    _____

    _____

    - How could we use context clues when we write?

    _____

    _____

    - How might we use context clues when we speak?

    _____

    _____

4. Share your ideas with the class.

Name: _____

Vocabulary: Context Clues

1. Read the paragraph below with a small group.

The tundra is the coldest biome. The temperature is below freezing for at least half of the year. We find this biome in the far north, not far from the polar ice caps. This biome also exists at the tops of very high mountains. Almost no trees grow there because the growing season is very short. Lichens, moss, grass, and shrubs grow there. They have adapted to the frozen ground. The top layer of soil thaws only a few inches down. The layer below that is always frozen. We call that layer *permafrost*. It does not rain much in the tundra, but it also does not warm up enough for water to evaporate. Parts of the tundra remain moist much of the year.

2. Underline any words that are new to you.

3. Use different-colored pencils, markers, or crayons to highlight any context clues that help you figure out each new word's meaning.

4. Work together to write context clues for each new word that doesn't already have at least one context clue. Use a dictionary and other resources to help you learn what the word means so you can write context clues. Write the new words and context clues on a separate piece of paper.

5. Work together with others in your group to write a paragraph about the tundra. Think about how you would answer the questions below for ideas. Write your paragraph on a separate piece of paper.

  ▪ What did you learn from reading the paragraph?

  ▪ What did you learn when you researched the new words?

  ▪ How can you include the context clues you wrote for #4 in your new paragraph?

6. Talk with others in your small group about how the context clues you included in your writing might help readers understand the information in your paragraph.

Name: _____

Vocabulary: Context Clues

WRITE

1. A travel guide gives people information about things to do and see in a certain place.

Research to learn about a biome that interests you. On a separate piece of paper, draw a graphic organizer similar to the example on the right. Note your sources in the box at the bottom. Your teacher may supply resources. ✎

Travel Guide

(name of place)

Fun Things to Do!

- _____
- _____
- _____
- _____

Interesting Things to See!

- _____
- _____
- _____
- _____

This is a great place to vacation because...

_____
_____
_____
_____

My Context Clues

Sources

2. Identify and learn the meanings of words that are new to you. Think about how you can include context clues in your writing to help readers understand what these words and ideas mean. Add your notes to your graphic organizer.

3. Follow the directions below to write a final copy of a travel guide page.

- Use your notes from the graphic organizer.
- Use complete sentences.
- Include context clues to help readers understand new words.
- Add color and graphics if you have time and space.

REFLECT

1. Use a separate piece of paper to complete the sentences below to review a classmate's travel guide.

- This travel guide catches my attention because _____.
- The things I would see or do if I visited this place are _____.
- The new words or ideas I learned reading this travel guide are _____.

2. Underline the context clues that helped you understand new words and ideas.

Name: _____

Vocabulary: Multiple-Meaning Words

Some words have more than one meaning. We call these **multiple-meaning words**. One way to tell which meaning a word has in a sentence is to look at how the word is used.

Example: Jeremy's uncle put some money in the *bank*.

Alexis played in the *bank* of snow.

1. Follow the tips below to go on a treasure hunt for multiple-meaning words.

    ▪ Look around the classroom for multiple-meaning words.

    ▪ Think about words you use in math.

    ▪ Think about words that name objects that also have another meaning.

    ▪ Think about words that name actions that also have another meaning.

    ▪ Think about words that have to do with nature or animals.

2. In the space below, draw a treasure chest. Write your words from #1 in the chest.

3. Share your words with classmates. Add any different words your classmates say to your treasure chest above.

4. Work together to create a chart similar to the sample below. Write your words and their meanings on chart paper or a whiteboard. An example has been done for you.

Word	Meaning #1	Meaning #2
bill	a piece of paper money	the beak of a bird

Name: _____

Vocabulary: Multiple-Meaning Words

1. Work with a small group to write sentences using multiple-meaning words you have learned. Use one multiple-meaning word in each sentence. Write two sentences for each word, one sentence for each meaning of the word. Mix up your sentences so that the multiple-meaning words are not printed one right after the other. Use a pencil.

   Example: Claire watched her mother write a *check* to the grocery store.

   Claire will *check* to make sure her lunch is in her backpack.

   _____

   _____

   _____

   _____

   _____

   _____

   _____

   _____

   _____

   _____

2. In the box below, write the multiple-meaning words you used.

3. Use a dark marker to cover up the multiple-meaning word in each sentence you wrote in #1 above.

4. Trade papers with another small group. Use the words in their word box to complete their sentences with the correct multiple-meaning words.

Name: _____

Vocabulary: Multiple-Meaning Words

WRITE

A riddle is a puzzling question that others answer by guessing. Work with a partner to write riddles for your classmates.

The answer to each of your riddles should be a single word that has more than one meaning.

Example: What is a layer of paint? *a coat*

What is a piece of clothing you wear to keep warm? *a coat*

Mix up your riddles so the two meanings of a word are not printed one right after the other. Do not write the answer next to each riddle.

_____

_____

_____

_____

_____

_____

REFLECT

1. Take turns sharing and guessing riddles with classmates.

2. Talk about what you learned about using multiple-meaning words by writing sentences and riddles in this lesson.

3. Read the statements below on your own. Write "true" or "false" on the line in front of each statement.

_____ We have to guess what a multiple-meaning word means in a sentence.

_____ All words have only one meaning.

_____ We can use a dictionary if we are not sure of the meaning(s) of a word.

_____ Multiple-meaning words may be used in different ways in a sentence.

_____ We learn multiple meanings of words to better understand what we read.

Name: _____

Vocabulary: Shades of Meaning

Some words mean almost the same thing, but they do not have exactly the same meaning. However, the words are connected.

When words have similar meanings, we say they have **shades of meaning**. We use these kinds of words to help us say exactly what we want to say. Some words have stronger meanings than others.

We can make our writing more descriptive when we think about the shades of meanings of different words. We can choose just the right word to make our writing clear and interesting.

Some verbs and adjectives have different shades of meaning. We use certain words to tell the mood or attitude of a person. These words describe *state of mind*. Other words help us describe how certain we are about something. We call this *degree of certainty*.

Examples: Keyona was <u>happy</u> to visit her friend on Saturday.

Carlos <u>thought</u> his friends might surprise him.

1. Talk with classmates about the first example that states Keyona's attitude (state of mind) about visiting her friend on Saturday. Follow the steps below to imagine different scenes.

   - Draw a semicircle on a separate piece of paper. Divide it into segments.

   - Brainstorm different words that might describe other thoughts, feelings, or attitudes Keyona might have about visiting her friend.

   - Talk about the situation or what might happen to make her have different states of mind about this event.

   - Write each word in a segment of your semicircle.

2. Talk about words that describe how certain we are about something. Use the second example to start your conversation. How certain is Carlos that his friends will surprise him? Write your ideas in the box below. Use a dictionary, thesaurus, or other resource as needed.

Name: _____

Vocabulary: Shades of Meaning

1. Work with a small group and follow the directions below to make word cards.

   ▪ Write one word on each slip of paper or cardstock.

   ▪ Start with the words you brainstormed in Learn #1 to describe states of mind. What other words describe states of mind? Use a print or online thesaurus for ideas. ⚡

   ▪ Add words you brainstormed in Learn #2 to describe degrees of certainty. What other words describe how certain someone is (or isn't) about something that might happen? Use a print or online thesaurus for ideas. ⚡

2. Trade your word cards with another small group.

3. Follow the directions below to participate in an activity.

   ▪ Mix up the word cards and put them all in one pile.

   ▪ Take turns drawing a card. State whether the word on your card describes a state of mind or a degree of certainty.

   ▪ Continue taking turns drawing cards until all of the cards have been drawn from the pile.

   ▪ Place your cards face up in front of you.

   ▪ Work with your group to separate the cards into two stacks: words that describe states of mind and words that describe degrees of certainty.

4. Write sentences about you and your friends. Or, write sentences about make-believe characters that are friends. Use the words on the cards you gathered during the activity in #3. Use a separate piece of paper if you need more space.

   _____

   _____

   _____

   _____

   _____

5. Share your sentences with others in your small group.

6. Talk about how using words that describe states of mind or degrees of certainty makes your writing more effective and interesting.

YOUR TURN

Name: _____

Vocabulary: Shades of Meaning

WRITE

1. Think about the questions below to brainstorm ideas to write about something you and a friend did together. Write your ideas on a separate piece of paper.

   ▪ What did you and your friend plan to do together?

   ▪ What did you think about the event or activity before you got together with your friend?

   ▪ How certain were you that it was going to happen the way you imagined?

   ▪ How did you feel about this event or activity before it happened?

   ▪ How did you feel about this event or activity after it was over?

2. Follow the tips below to write a narrative about what you and your friend did together. Use a separate piece of paper.

   ▪ Introduce the situation, including the setting and characters.

   ▪ Use dialogue and description to tell what you and your friend said, did, thought, and felt during the experience.

   ▪ Describe events within the experience in an order that makes sense.

   ▪ Write a final sentence that describes how the experience ended.

REFLECT

1. Trade narratives with a partner.

2. In the boxes below, write words your partner used that have shades of meaning. Which words described their *states of mind* (how they thought or felt about something)? Which words described *degrees of certainty* (how certain they were that something would happen the way they thought or planned)?

States of Mind	Degrees of Certainty

Name: _____

Figurative Language: Idioms

Figurative language helps make reading and writing more interesting. We use language in different ways. Literal language uses the exact meaning of a word or words.

Example: The literal meaning of "wind" is air that moves.

Figurative language uses words in ways different from their literal meaning. It tells an idea in an interesting way.

Example: The figurative meaning of "to get wind of something" is to hear a rumor about something.

Some phrases don't mean exactly the same as what the words mean. We call these **idioms**. The figurative meaning of the phrase in the second example is an idiom. An idiom is a group of words that has a different, or figurative, meaning from the exact meaning of each word in the phrase. Sometimes, the words in an idiom give us clues about its meaning.

Idioms make our writing more interesting. Sometimes, there is not one exact word to say what we mean. It would take too many words if we used the literal meanings of words. We might be able to use an idiom that has a figurative meaning.

1. Read the sample sentences below. Think about the literal meaning of the underlined words. These words form an idiom. When we say them together, they have a different meaning. Write what you think is the figurative meaning of the underlined words in each sentence. Use a separate piece of paper.

   ▪ Samantha said she felt <u>under the weather</u> yesterday.

   ▪ The directions to the store left me <u>in a fog</u>.

   ▪ Our neighbor stomped across the yard with <u>a face like thunder</u>.

2. Talk about each idiom one at a time with classmates. Share your ideas about what each idiom means. Together, answer the questions below.

   ▪ How did you figure out the meaning for each idiom?

   ▪ How did context clues in the sentences help you figure out the meanings of the idioms?

   ▪ What other sample sentences can you think of that use one of these idioms, or another idiom about weather?

PRACTICE

Name: _____

Figurative Language: Idioms

1. Work with a small group to write what you think the idiom in each sentence means. Use context clues and what you have experienced and know about weather.

▪ Emily was on <u>cloud nine</u> when she saw her report card.

_____

▪ Grandma always said, "<u>Every cloud has a silver lining</u>."

_____

_____

▪ Anthony felt <u>right as rain</u> about the gift he chose for his brother.

_____

▪ Liam put some money in his piggy bank <u>for a rainy day</u>.

_____

▪ It's <u>raining cats and dogs</u>, so we'll have to play inside.

_____

2. Work together to write your own sentences using each idiom.

_____

_____

_____

_____

_____

_____

3. What other idiom can you think of that is related to the weather? Work together to write another new sentence on a separate piece of paper. Draw a picture to go with your sentence.

4. Share your new sentences from #2 and #3 with classmates.

Name: _____

Figurative Language: Idioms

WRITE

1. Follow the steps below to brainstorm ideas for a silly story about weather. Use a separate piece of paper.

   ▪ Draw an umbrella.

   ▪ Add clouds and other weather pictures to your drawing.

   ▪ Add the character(s) who will be in your story.

   ▪ Write a sentence in the bottom-left corner. Tell a problem the character(s) have or describe what they want.

   ▪ Write a sentence in the bottom-right corner. Tell how the character(s) solve the problem.

2. Write your story on a separate piece of paper. Use idioms to make your writing interesting. Make sure the idioms make sense in the story.

REFLECT

1. Trade stories with a partner.

2. Use the checklist below to decide how effectively your partner used idioms in their writing.

   ☐ The story has at least one idiom.

   ☐ Each idiom is a phrase that has a figurative meaning separate from the literal meaning of the words.

   ☐ The idioms make the writing more interesting.

   ☐ Each idiom conveys an idea clearly.

   ☐ Each idiom is used correctly in a way that makes sense.

3. Talk with classmates about the questions below.

   ▪ Why do we use idioms in our talking and writing?

   ▪ Why do idioms often sound funny?

   ▪ How can we use idioms to communicate exactly what we want to say and make our writing more interesting?

Name: _____

Figurative Language: Symbolism

Figurative language uses words in ways different from their basic meaning. It tells an idea in an interesting way.

We use symbols in figurative language. A **symbol** is a thing, an action, or an event that represents a certain thing or idea. When we use a word or phrase as a symbol, the symbol reflects the figurative meaning of the picture, object, idea, or feeling.

We use symbols to help readers connect to a story. Symbols also help readers think about what the author wants to say.

Examples: The man wore a purple robe and a crown.

I lay on the soft, green grass and watched wispy clouds float across the bright blue sky.

1. The color words in each example above symbolize an idea. Talk with classmates about the ideas and meaning of the color words used in the examples.
   - What information does the word *purple* give us about the man?
   - How would you describe the scene in the second example? Why?

2. Listen as your teacher reads a poem aloud. Your teacher can find poem titles in the Answer Key. 🗯

3. Draw a picture of what the poet describes as you listen to your teacher read the poem a second time. If you need more room, use a separate piece of paper. 🗯

4. Share your drawing with classmates. Use the questions below to talk together about symbols we use in writing.
   - What colors or other symbols did the poet use in the poem?
   - What ideas or feelings did the symbols represent in the poem?
   - What colors have you seen used as symbols when you read poems and stories, especially folk tales or fairy tales?
   - What other objects do we often find used as symbols in poems and stories?
   - What do these things often represent?

Name: _____

Figurative Language: Symbolism

1. Work with a small group to list ideas and feelings we might want to represent with symbols. Complete the left column of the chart below. An example has been done for you.

Ideas and Feelings	Color	Meaning or Author's Message
friendship	yellow	We may think of yellow as a happy color; some people use yellow to show playfulness or warmth, which are both feelings we think of when we think of friendship.

2. Trade papers with another small group. What colors would you use to stand for the ideas and feelings your classmates listed? Think about how an author might use these ideas and feelings in a story or poem. In the center column of the chart above, list a color for each idea or feeling. An example has been done for you.

3. Trade papers again with another small group. Read your classmates' notes in the left and center columns of the chart. Think about the questions below to complete the chart. Write your ideas in the right column. An example has been done for you.

   ▪ What colors did your classmates note that an author might use as symbols for the ideas and feelings in the left column?

   ▪ What meanings do you think the colors express?

   ▪ What meanings might the ideas and feelings have in a poem or story?

4. Answer the questions below with classmates to talk about how we use colors as symbols to add meaning to writing.

   ▪ How did you choose colors to stand for each idea or feeling?

   ▪ How did thinking about a color symbol for each idea or feeling help you think about what an author might want to say about that idea or feeling?

YOUR TURN

Name: _____

Figurative Language: Symbolism

WRITE

1. Answer the questions below to think about how you might use color to represent ideas and feelings in your writing.

   ▪ What is your favorite color? Why? _____

   _____

   ▪ In your mind, what does that color represent? Why? _____

   _____

   ▪ How could you use that color to add meaning to your writing? _____

   _____

2. Use your answers to the questions above to brainstorm an idea for a story or poem. Use the graphic organizer below to plan.

Main Idea		Color Symbol	
Character or Narrator	**Events**		**Sensory Details**

REFLECT

1. Write a journal entry to explain how you could use colors as symbols in a story or poem. Use a separate piece of paper.

2. Talk about your journal entry with a partner. Ask and answer questions about your ideas to better understand how we use symbols in our writing.

3. Work together to write one or more statements about how to use symbols to add meaning to writing. Use the same separate piece of paper.

4. Share your statements with the class.

Name: _____

Figurative Language: Personification

Figurative language uses words in ways different from their basic meaning. It tells an idea in an interesting way.

Sometimes, we give an object or animal the qualities of a person. We call this **personification**.

Example: The car complained as it went up the hill.

People complain. A car does not literally complain; the engine makes noise.

1. Talk with classmates about movies you have watched in which an object or animal has characteristics or behaves like a person.

2. Work together to complete the chart below. An example has been done for you.

Movie Title	Object or Animal	Characteristics or Behaviors
Pinocchio	A piece of wood is made into a wooden puppet.	The wood talks and acts like a boy.

3. Read the questions below and write your ideas on a separate piece of paper.

   ▪ How do movie creators or book authors use personification to tell a story?

   ▪ How does personification help the audience understand the story?

   ▪ How does personification add meaning to what is happening?

   ▪ How does personification make a story more interesting?

4. Talk with classmates about the answers you wrote for #3.

Name: _____

Figurative Language: Personification

1. Work with a small group to study <u>Alice in Wonderland</u>. Read a print or online picture book copy of the story, or watch a clip from the movie. Your teacher will provide this. 📝

2. Look for examples of personification as you study the story, and write them in the chart below.

Object or Animal	Characteristics or Behaviors

3. Work together with your group. Use your notes from the chart to answer the questions below about the personification in this story.

   ▪ What is one example of personification you noticed in the story?

   _____

   _____

   ▪ How would this part of the story be different if the author had not included personification?

   _____

   _____

   _____

   ▪ In general, how does personification add to the story?

   _____

   _____

4. Share your responses to #3 with another group.

Name: _____

Figurative Language: Personification

WRITE

1. Answer the questions below to imagine what it would be like if a familiar object came to life. It might be a toy, something you use at school, or an object you use every day at home.

   ▪ What is the object? _____

   ▪ What human characteristics or behaviors will this object have?

   _____

   ▪ How would you interact with this object?

   _____

   ▪ What story problem could you solve with this object?

   _____

   _____

2. Write a narrative to describe what happens when this object comes to life. Use a separate piece of paper.

REFLECT

1. Trade narratives with a partner. Color the rectangle next to each statement that best describes your partner's writing.

	Expert	Good	Still Learning
An object or animal talks or acts like a person.			
The personification tells what the author wants to say in an interesting way.			
The personification makes the writing stronger and more descriptive.			

2. Think about how you would answer the questions below to review this lesson with a partner.

   ▪ Which movies did you talk about with classmates in Learn #2?

   ▪ Which characteristics or behaviors did you and other classmates note in Practice #2?

   ▪ How did the personification examples you studied add detail to stories and make descriptions stronger?

Name: _____

Figurative Language: Similes and Metaphors

A **simile** makes a comparison between two things using a comparison word (*like* or *as*).

Examples: The <u>decks</u> were like a <u>slide</u>, where a seaman scarce could stand.

The frost was on the village roofs as <u>white</u> as <u>ocean foam</u>.

We use similes in our writing to make it more interesting. Similes give readers a mental picture and help them understand what we are describing.

A **metaphor** compares two things without using a comparison word. These things are often different, but the metaphor compares them as if they are the same.

Examples: The ocean is the heart of Earth's climate.

The sea is history.

1. With classmates, read a poem about the ocean. Your teacher can find poem titles in the Answer Key. !

2. Answer the questions below as you talk about the poem with classmates.

   ▪ How did the author compare the ocean to something else in the poem?

   ▪ What is the author's message in the poem?

3. Follow the steps below to describe your understanding of the poem.

   ▪ Work with a small group. Assign each person in the group one of the five senses.

   ▪ Think about how the author described the ocean in the poem.

   ▪ What would you compare the ocean to using the sense you were assigned? Write your answer on a separate piece of paper.

   ▪ Use the sense you were assigned to write a simile or metaphor to compare the ocean to something else for someone who perhaps has not experienced or visited the ocean. Write your simile or metaphor on the same separate piece of paper.

4. Share your answers to #3 above with others in your small group. Using your answers, complete a web similar to the example on the right.

5. Talk with classmates about how your similes and metaphors might help readers visualize the ocean.

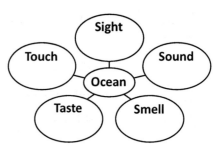

Name: _____

Figurative Language: Similes and Metaphors

1. Look at the photographs below.

2. What does each photo remind you of?

① _____   ③ _____

② _____   ④ _____

3. Write a simile or metaphor to compare something in each photograph with the object, idea, or experience you noted in #2 above. Use a separate piece of paper and number your similes and metaphors to match the photographs.

4. Follow the steps below to compare your similes and metaphors with classmates' writing in a small group.

- List the image pictured in each numbered photograph in the second column of the chart below.

- In the third column, list the things your classmates compared to each photograph.

	Image in Photograph	Compared to
1		
2		
3		
4		

Name: _____

Figurative Language: Similes and Metaphors

WRITE

1. Think about a body of water in your community or some place you have visited. This might be the ocean, a lake, a river, or a pond. Name the body of water.

_____

2. How would you describe that body of water for someone who has not seen it?

_____

_____

3. What can you compare to this body of water to help others visualize it?

_____

4. Write a simile to compare this body of water to something else. Use a comparison word (*like* or *as*) in your simile.

_____

_____

5. Write a metaphor to compare this body of water to something else. Remember, a metaphor compares two different things as though they are the same.

_____

_____

REFLECT

1. Talk with a partner about the simile and metaphor you wrote in Write #4 and #5. Ask them for help to revise your sentences as needed so your writing makes sense and is clear and easy to understand.

2. Trade papers with a different partner and complete the sentence frames below.

   ▪ Your simile works well because _____.

   ▪ Your metaphor compares a(n) _____ to a(n) _____.

   ▪ Your metaphor suggests these two things are similar because _____

   _____.

Name: _____

Figurative Language: Analogies

An **analogy** is a relationship between words. It is a comparison between two things. When we make analogies, we think about how words and ideas connect to other words and ideas.

When we make an analogy, we first look at two words that relate to each other in some way. Then we look at a third word and try to think of a word that relates to it in the same way the first two words relate to each other.

Example: moon : night :: sun : day

We read the analogy above by saying "moon is to night as sun is to day."

Learning how to make analogies helps us think about how to compare two objects, actions, or ideas. We can use the word relationship in an analogy to then write similes and metaphors to describe things in interesting ways in our writing.

1. Read the steps below with classmates to learn how to make analogies.
   - Look at the first two items in the first analogy in #2 below.
   - Work together to state how those two items are connected. Describe the relationship between the two items.
   - Think of two other items (things or ideas) that have a similar relationship.

2. Use the steps above to practice completing the analogies below.
   - up: down :: _____ : _____
   - roller coaster: ride :: _____ : _____

3. In the second row of the chart below, write two items or ideas that are connected in some way. Write your ideas in columns A and B.

A	B	C	D

4. Ask a classmate to complete the analogy. They will write two words that have a similar relationship in columns C and D in the second row.

5. Take turns with classmates to write the first and second word relationships in an analogy in the chart. Write the first set of word relationships in columns A and B. Write the similar (second) set of word relationships in columns C and D.

Name: _____

Figurative Language: Analogies

1. Work with a small group of three other classmates.

2. Brainstorm words that connect to each other in different ways (synonyms, antonyms, part/whole, cause/effect, thing/use, thing/characteristic, category/subcategory, fact/opinion, problem/solution). Think of words that have to do with a fair or an amusement park. Write your ideas in the box below.

_____

3. Follow the steps below to write analogies with your group. Use the words you wrote in #2 for ideas.

   ▪ The first person says a word to start the sentence frame.

   _____ is to _____ as _____ is to _____.

   ▪ The next person compares the first word to something that relates in some way.

   ▪ The third person continues the analogy by saying a word that connects to the first word.

   ▪ The fourth person finishes the analogy with a word that connects to the second word in the same way the first two words relate to each other.

4. Check your analogy. Does it make sense? Do the words connect to each other in a way that compares two objects, actions, or ideas?

5. Work together to write three more analogies as described above.

   ▪ _____ is to _____ as _____ is to _____.

   ▪ _____ is to _____ as _____ is to _____.

   ▪ _____ is to _____ as _____ is to _____.

6. Work together to write similes or metaphors using the words and ideas from your analogies. Write your similes or metaphors on a separate piece of paper.

7. Talk about how you could use your similes and metaphors to write about an experience at a fair or an amusement park.

8. On your own, write about the experience you described in #7. Use a separate piece of paper.

Name: _____

Figurative Language: Analogies

WRITE

Analogies compare two or more things or ideas. Similes and metaphors also compare things, often using descriptive words. An analogy explains the topic to help readers better understand. We might use an analogy in opinion and informative writing. However, we use similes and metaphors more often in narrative or poetic writing.

1. Choose an analogy you have made in this lesson about amusement parks and answer the questions below.

    ▪ What did you compare in the analogy?

    _____

    _____

    ▪ How do these things remind you of each other?

    _____

    _____

    ▪ How would you explain the relationship between these ideas?

    _____

    _____

2. Use your notes above to write an informative paragraph about part of an amusement park, or your experience visiting an amusement park. Make an analogy in your paragraph to help readers better understand your ideas. Write your paragraph on a separate piece of paper.

REFLECT

1. Answer the questions below to review what you have learned about making and using analogies in your writing. Use a separate piece of paper.

    ▪ What are analogies?

    ▪ How do we use analogies in our writing?

    ▪ Why do we use analogies?

2. Share your notes from Reflect #1 with a partner and rehearse how you would explain analogies to a friend or family member.

Name: _____

Figurative Language: Alliteration and Onomatopoeia

We use words to tell about an idea or to say how we feel. Sometimes, our words are poems. When we write a poem, we choose words for their sound and meaning. We think about how the words flow. Poems use language in different ways.

One way we use language in poems is to use words that have first letters that sound the same. We call this **alliteration**.

Example: The blue bug bit a big black bear.

1. Follow the tips below to research examples of alliteration with classmates. Your teacher may supply resources. 📛
    - Look at online or print copies of Mother Goose rhymes.
    - Research and read tongue-twisters.

2. With classmates, brainstorm words related to nature. Record the words on chart paper or a whiteboard. Which words begin with the same letter? Which synonyms could you add that begin with the same letter as one or more words you already have written?

3. Work together to write phrases that use alliteration. Your phrases may be about nature. They may be silly. Practice saying the phrases aloud to see how alliteration affects the sound of what we write and read. Write your phrases on chart paper or a whiteboard.

Another way we use language in poems is to use words that sound like what the word means. We call this **onomatopoeia**.

Example: I heard an owl *hoot* in the woods.

1. Circle the words in the box below that fit the description of onomatopoeia. Which words sound like their meaning?

animal	boom	cliff	earth	leaves	ribbit
baa	bush	clip-clop	eek	meow	splat
bark	buzz	cluck	huh	moo	squawk
barn	chomp	crash	hum	park	tree
beep	clang	desert	lake	playground	woof

2. Take turns reading the words aloud with classmates to check your work.

Name: _____

Figurative Language: Alliteration and Onomatopoeia

1. Review the words you brainstormed in Learn #2 (the first activity) that show alliteration.

2. Work with a small group to talk about an idea or message you would like to say in a poem.

3. Write a sentence about nature. Include some words in your sentence that begin with the same letter.

   _____

   _____

4. Share your sentence with your small group. Work together to combine all of your sentences into a poem. Write your poem on a separate piece of paper.

5. Read your poem and answer the questions below.

   ▪ Which parts of the poem have natural rhythm?

   _____

   _____

   ▪ Which lines would you revise so they flow better with the rest of the poem?

   _____

   _____

   ▪ How could you revise those lines?

   _____

   _____

6. Follow the steps below to publish and present your poem.

   ▪ Rewrite your poem on a separate piece of paper with any changes you described in #5 above. Use alliteration in your poem.

   ▪ Practice reading your poem together as a group.

   ▪ Read your poem aloud together and make a recording.

   ▪ Work together to create one or more drawings to illustrate your poem.

   ▪ Present your recording and illustrations to the class.

Name: _____

Figurative Language: Alliteration and Onomatopoeia

WRITE

1. Answer the questions below about your favorite place in nature. Write your answers on a separate piece of paper.

   - What is your favorite place outdoors? Why?

   - What do you hear when you visit this place? What words can you use to describe those sounds? Review Learn #1 (the second activity) for ideas.

   - What do you see when you visit this place?

   - What do you smell or taste when you visit this place?

   - What do you touch when you visit this place?

2. How can you use alliteration to write about your favorite outdoor place? Use a thesaurus to find synonyms that begin with the same letter(s) for the words you wrote in answer to the questions in #1. List words you could use to create alliteration below.

   ┌───┐
   │   │
   │   │
   │   │
   │   │
   └───┘

3. Write a poem about your favorite outdoor place. Use onomatopoeia and alliteration in your poem. Include sensory details. Write your poem on a separate piece of paper.

REFLECT

1. Trade poems and papers with a partner, and whisper-read your partner's poem.

2. Use a colored pencil, crayon, or marker to highlight words in the poem that show onomatopoeia.

3. Use a different-colored pencil, crayon, or marker to highlight words in your partner's poem that create alliteration.

4. Complete the sentence frame below to offer feedback to your partner.

   I could visualize your favorite outdoor place because _____

   _____.

5. Talk about your answer to #4 with your partner. Explain how their use of onomatopoeia and alliteration added to your understanding of their poem.

Name: _____

Figurative Language: Hyperbole

We use words to say how we feel or to tell about an idea. Sometimes, our words are poems. When we write a poem, we choose words for their sound and meaning. We think about how the words flow. We also use poetic language to add richness and meaning to prose. *Prose* is writing that uses complete sentences, not written in verse or as poetry.

Hyperbole is an exaggeration used for humor or emphasis. We use hyperbole for effect or to make writing more interesting. Readers recognize the exaggeration is not true; it is used to make a point. We usually use hyperbole in stories or poetry.

Examples: We climbed a gigantic mountain that touched the sky.

Riding dirt bikes is all he ever wants to do.

1. Eating a hearty breakfast is an important beginning to an extreme adventure. Read the excerpt below about Paul Bunyan to learn how breakfast is served in the logging camp.

   Feeding Paul Bunyan's crews wasn't an easy job. It was never quite the same at each camp. The winter he logged off North Dakota, he had 300 cooks. They made pancakes for the seven axemen and the little chore-boy. The cooking didn't go too well at the next camp. After that, Paul hired his cousin Big Joe. He was the only man who could make pancakes fast enough to feed the crew. He had Big Ole, the blacksmith, make him a griddle. It was so big you couldn't see across it when the steam was thick. The batter was stirred in drums like concrete mixers. Then Big Joe poured it on the griddle with cranes and spouts. The griddle was greased by boys who skated over the surface with hams tied to their feet.

2. Underline any examples of hyperbole in the paragraph you read in #1. Share what you underlined with classmates.

3. Answer the questions below with classmates. Write your answers on chart paper or a whiteboard.
   - What is hyperbole?
   - How can we use hyperbole in our writing?
   - Why do we use hyperbole in writing?

4. Work together to create a list of tips for using hyperbole in your writing.

Name: _____

Figurative Language: Hyperbole

1. As a class, brainstorm and decide on an extreme adventure you will use as your topic for this activity. Write a phrase or sentence to describe the adventure.

   _____

   _____

2. In a group of five, count off one through five so that each person in the group has a number. This will be your study group number.

3. Meet with other classmates who have the same study number you have. Work together to answer the numbered question below that matches your study group number. Highlight or draw a star next to the question your study group will answer.

   ① What part of the adventure is most important or meaningful to you?

   ② How would you describe an important part of the adventure?

   ③ How would you describe certain qualities connected to an important part of the adventure (for example, the size of something, difficulty of a task, appearance of something you see, characteristic of something you hear, smell, or touch)?

   ④ How could you describe an important part of the adventure in a creative way?

   ⑤ How could you exaggerate one quality of an important part of the adventure?

4. Take notes from your study group's conversation about your assigned question.

   _____

   _____

   _____

   _____

   _____

5. Meet with the same group you started with in #2 above.

6. Take turns sharing your answers to the numbered questions, beginning with question #1.

7. If you have time, work together to write a paragraph describing a scene from the extreme adventure named in #1 above. Use hyperbole in your description. Write your paragraph on a separate piece of paper.

Name: _____

Figurative Language: Hyperbole

WRITE

1. Follow the tips below to plan a story about an extreme adventure.

   ▪ Think of sports or activities you like to do.

   ▪ Think of something related to this sport or activity that would be daring, challenging, or unusual.

   ▪ Look at photographs of the sport or activity for ideas. Your teacher may help you find some. ⚡

2. Write your extreme adventure topic in the starburst below.

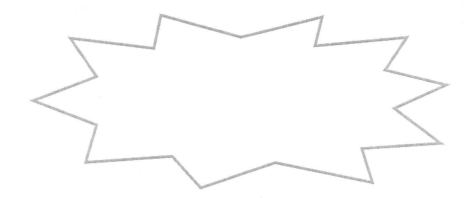

3. Around the starburst, write qualities or characteristics of the adventure.

4. Write a paragraph to describe the extreme adventure. Use hyperbole in your writing. Write your paragraph on a separate piece of paper.

REFLECT

1. Trade this page and your paragraph with a partner's.

2. Use the following checklist to describe how effectively they used hyperbole in their paragraphs. Write a checkmark in the column that best illustrates their writing.

	Good job!	Keep practicing
The paragraph uses hyperbole to make a point.		
The hyperbole makes the writing more interesting.		
The hyperbole exaggerates a characteristic or quality of some part of the extreme adventure.		

Answer Key

Nouns: Plural, Regular and Irregular (pages 5–7)
Learn
1. geese; peaches
2. Answers:
   ⓐ loaves ⓑ leaves, pieces, heads
3. Answers:
   ⓐ Sentence should use _bison_ correctly.
   ⓑ Sentence should use _cherries_ correctly.

Pronouns: Subject and Object (pages 8–10)
Learn
1. Sample answers:
   ▪ I, you, he, she, it; me, you, him, her, it
   ▪ we, you, they; us, you, them
   ▪ group by singular and plural; group by subject and object
Your Turn (Reflect)
2. Sample answers:
   ▪ subject and object pronouns
   ▪ Pronouns replace nouns in sentences.
   ▪ Pronouns give writing more variety and make it flow more smoothly.

Subject-Verb Agreement (pages 14–16)
Learn
2. Sample answers:
   ▪ We (2+) study (P)
   ▪ California condors (2+) have (P)
   ▪ wings (2+) are (P)
   ▪ Chinese giant salamander (1) is (S)
   ▪ It (1) weighs (S)
   ▪ monkeys and baboons (2+) live (P)

Conjunctions: Coordinating (pages 23–25)
Learn
1. Answers: and, or, and, but
2. Sample answers: In the second sentence, the coordinating conjunctions _and_ and _or_ join words. In the fifth sentence, the coordinating conjunction _and_ joins words. In the last sentence, _but_ joins two independent clauses.
Practice
1. Sample topics: animals—snails, slugs, frogs; materials—garden mud, cement mud, volcanic mud pots

Conjunctions: Subordinating (pages 26–28)
Learn
3. Sample answers:
   ▪ when, that, because
   ▪ First sentence: a cause-and-effect relationship that shows time; second sentence: place relationship; third sentence: a reason to support the statement
   ▪ First sentence: comma used after introductory dependent clause; second and third sentences: no comma needed because both of the clauses can stand on their own
   ▪ Subordinating conjunctions make the sentences flow smoothly and add meaning.

Sentences: Simple (pages 29–31)
Learn
2. Answers:
   ⓐ simple subject; simple predicate
   ⓑ compound subject; simple predicate
   ⓒ simple subject; simple predicate
   ⓓ simple subject; compound predicate

3. Sample answers:
   ▪ "On a trampoline" tells where Gabe jumped; "on his birthday" tells when he jumped.
   ▪ "To their birthday party" tells what the subject invited the object (Avery) to.
   ▪ "Every year" tells when the subject marks his height; "his height" tells what the subject marks; "on a growth chart" tells where he makes the marks.
   ▪ "Pictures" and "their names" tells what the children drew and signed; "on a card" tells where they drew and signed; "for their teacher" tells the object (who will receive the action of the drawing and signing).
   ▪ About word order: the subjects come before the verbs.

Sentences: Compound (pages 32–34)
Learn
3. Sample answers:
   ▪ It would sound choppy and unnatural.
   ▪ Compound sentences add meaning and interest to a story.

Sentences: Complex (pages 35–37)
Practice
4. Sample answers:
   ▪ Our sentences are complex sentences because they each have an independent clause and a dependent clause.
   ▪ I have learned that complex sentences often have a subordinating conjunction that introduces the dependent clause.

Run-on Sentences and Sentence Fragments (pages 38–40)
Learn
3. Sample answer: Rewrite sentences as separate sentences with correct punctuation. Also, see tips listed for Practice #4.
Practice
2. Sample answers: Run-on sentences are underlined; sentence fragments are in bold.
Machines and equipment can break in space there is not always room to bring more parts and tools to fix things astronauts need to find solutions to such problems. **One way to fix a machine.** They might use a 3D printer to create parts for a certain mission. **Astronauts. Still need to understand. 3D printing works when.** An experiment on board the space station is studying small bits of material that can come together like building blocks to make certain things scientists use the bits of material to make other things to meet their needs.

Capitalization: Titles (pages 41–43)
Learn
1. Answers:
   ▪ the jungle book
   ▪ call of the wild
   ▪ the little red hen
   ▪ homeward bound
   ▪ because of winn-dixie
   ▪ doctor dolittle
   ▪ three blind mice
   ▪ mary had a little lamb

Punctuation: Addresses (pages 44–46)
Learn
3. The city and state names in #1 are separated by a comma; the street, city, and state names in #2 are separated by commas.

Answer Key *(cont.)*

Your Turn (Reflect)
1. Answers:
   - An address tells us the street, city, and state of a place. We can then use a map to get to the place.
   - We might write addresses in an address book or type them into a smartphone's address book.
   - Sometimes, two streets are similar; with correct spelling, we will get to the right place. We use capital letters for proper nouns so that we know this is the name of a certain place.
   - Correct punctuation sets the city and state names apart so we can tell the difference between the two.

Punctuation: Possessives (pages 47–49)
Learn
2. Harriet's seven brothers, Harriet's political views, Harriet's father and husband, Harriet's book, Uncle Tom's Cabin, Harriet's writing

Punctuation: Dialogue (pages 50–52)
Your Turn (Reflect)
1. Answers:
   - We use quotation marks to show what someone said.
   - In a story or scene, the words someone says are called dialogue.
   - The first word in a quotation is always capitalized.
   - We use a comma to set off the exact words of a speaker from the rest of the sentence.

Types of Writing: Informative (pages 56–58)
Learn
2. Sample answers:
   - *Who?* No certain person is mentioned.
   - *What?* Vehicles ride on a cushion of air.
   - *When?* A certain time is not mentioned; past tense verbs tell about the first hovercraft in the past. Present tense verbs tell about hovercraft now.
   - *Where?* English Channel, southern England, northern France
   - *Why?* They transport people and cars; many are used for sport and military purposes.
   - *How?* They ride on a cushion of air; paragraph is not long enough to give other details about how.

Formal and Informal English (pages 62–64)
Learn
2. Sample answers: formal English—"focus," has no contractions, complete sentences, and a formal tone
4. Sample answers: informal English—"Hey," "u," "gonna," "cool," "lots," "lotta," has contractions and an informal tone

Vocabulary: Synonyms and Antonyms (pages 65–67)
Learn
1. Sample answers: abode, home, shelter, ranch, cottage, farmhouse, apartment, hut, condo, castle, mansion, cabin, tent, townhouse

Vocabulary: Words and Phrases for Effect (pages 68–70)
Practice
2. Sample answers:
   - Mowgli shows off and teases Baloo.
   - Baloo is hurt yet still cares for Mowgli.
   - Answers will vary.

4. Sample answers: sullen, very angry (Mowgli's dialogue), hurt and grieved, delighted to show off, applaud himself, drumming with his heels, glossy skin, worst faces, tenderly

Vocabulary: Root Words and Prefixes (pages 71–73)
Learn
2. Sample answer (second bullet): context clues, break a word down to the root word, think about words I know and what they mean, use a dictionary

Vocabulary: Root Words and Suffixes (pages 74–76)
Learn
2. Answers: restless, delightful, useful, gently, helpless, messy
3. Sample answers:
   - *Rest* (root) is a verb; *restless* is an adjective that describes a person who is without rest or is not resting.
   - *Delight* (root) is a noun; *delightful* is an adjective that describes a person or thing that is full of delight or charm.
   - *Use* (root) is a verb; *useful* is an adjective that describes a person or thing that is full of use or is able to be used.
   - *Gentle* (root) is an adjective; *gently* is an adverb that describes a mild or tender manner.
   - *Help* (root) is a verb; *helpless* is an adjective that describes a person or thing that cannot help itself.
   - *Mess* (root) is a noun; *messy* is an adjective that describes a person or thing that is untidy or dirty.

Vocabulary: Context Clues (pages 77–79)
Learn
2. Sample answer: The sentences give clues about the word biome—a large, natural community or environment where plants and animals live.
3. Sample answers:
   - Context clues help us figure out the meanings of new words so we can better understand what we read.
   - We can include context clues when we write to help our readers better understand what we are trying to say. We can use other words in a sentence to define a new word. We can use synonyms or antonyms. We can explain the meaning of a word in the sentence before or after the sentence that has the new word.
   - We can include context clues to help listeners understand any new words we choose to use when we speak.

Vocabulary: Multiple-Meaning Words (pages 80–82)
Your Turn (Reflect)
3. Answers:
   - False; we should be able to tell the meaning of a multiple-meaning word by the way it is used in a sentence.
   - False; some words have more than one meaning.
   - True
   - True; multiple-meaning words can function as different parts of speech (for example, *wave* is a noun meaning a long body of water that curls and breaks on shore, and *wave* is a verb that means to move one's hand back and forth as a signal).
   - True; understanding multiple-meaning words increases overall vocabulary, which leads to better reading comprehension.

Answer Key *(cont.)*

Figurative Language: Idioms (pages 86–88)
Learn
1. Sample answers:
   - under the weather: somewhat ill or gloomy
   - in a fog: confused
   - a face like thunder: angry or upset about something

Practice
1. Sample answers:
   - on cloud nine: very happy
   - every cloud has a silver lining: there is always something good even in an unpleasant, difficult, or painful situation
   - right as rain: perfectly fine
   - for a rainy day: possible future time of hardship
   - raining cats and dogs: raining very hard
3. Sample answers: chasing rainbows; come rain or shine; when it rains it pours; weather the storm

Your Turn (Reflect)
3. Sample answers:
   - We use idioms in our talking and writing to make our ideas interesting and to help our audience understand exactly what we want to say.
   - Idioms often sound funny because the words have a different meaning from their literal, or exact, meaning. An idiom might not make sense if we consider only the literal meanings of the words.
   - We can use idioms to communicate exactly what we want to say by using a group of words that has a figurative meaning. Idioms make our writing more interesting by saying something in a different way. We can use idioms when there is not one exact word to say what we want to say.

Figurative Language: Symbolism (pages 89–91)
Learn
1. Sample answers:
   - Often, *purple* stands for royalty. This color, along with the word *crown*, tells readers the man may be a king.
   - The colors *green* and *blue* are cool colors, giving the impression of peace, calm, and rest. The person describing the scene may feel relaxed and peaceful.
2. Sample poems:
   - "The Eagle" by Alfred Lord Tennyson
   - "XXXV (A man saw a ball of gold in the sky)" (first stanza in particular) by Stephen Crane
   - "My Heart Leaps Up When I Behold" by William Wordsworth
   - "What Is Pink?" by Christina Rossetti

Figurative Language: Personification (pages 92–94)
Learn
3. Sample answers:
   - Movie creators or book authors use personification to give something that isn't human the qualities of a person. This makes the animal or thing seem like an actual character in the story.
   - Personification helps an audience understand a story by making it easier for them to connect with the object or animal. Describing something with human characteristics helps readers understand or sympathize with the character. Personification gives an audience a mental picture.
   - Personification can add meaning to what is happening by showing how a character feels about an object. It adds meaning by adding detail to a story.
   - Personification makes a story more interesting because it adds vivid description and feelings to the writing.

Practice
2. Sample answers:
   - The White Rabbit looks at his pocket watch.
   - The playing cards are soldiers, gardeners, royalty, and members of the court.
   - The pieces in the croquet game come to life.
   - The Gryphon and Mock Turtle dance.
   - Animals throughout the story talk.

Figurative Language: Similes and Metaphors (pages 95–97)
Learn
1. Sample poems:
   - "Sea Calm" by Langston Hughes
   - "Young Sea" by Carl Sandburg
   - "At the Sea-Side" by Robert Louis Stevenson

Figurative Language: Analogies (pages 98–100)
Learn
2. Sample answers:
   - up: down :: [words that are opposites]
   - roller coaster: ride :: [words that describe something that is part of a larger group or type]

Your Turn (Reflect)
1. Sample answers:
   - Analogies are comparisons between words and ideas that have a relationship with each other.
   - We use analogies in our writing by comparing two things or ideas and showing a relationship or connection.
   - We use analogies to explain ideas so readers can better understand a topic.

Figurative Language: Alliteration and Onomatopoeia
(pages 101–103)
Learn (Part 2)
1. Circle these words: baa, bark, beep, boom, buzz, chomp, clang, clip-clop, cluck, crash, eek, huh, hum, meow, moo, ribbit, splat, squawk, woof

Figurative Language: Hyperbole (pages 104–106)
Learn
2. Sample answers:
   - he had 300 cooks
   - He was the only man who could make pancakes fast enough to feed the crew.
   - It was so big you couldn't see across it when the steam was thick.
   - The batter was stirred in drums like concrete mixers.
   - Big Joe poured it on with cranes and spouts
   - The griddle was greased by boys who skated over the surface with hams tied to their feet.
3. Sample answers:
   - Hyperbole is an exaggeration used for humor or emphasis.
   - We use hyperbole by exaggerating a quality or detail in a story.
   - We use hyperbole to make a point, for effect, and to make writing more interesting.

Meeting Standards

Each unit meets one or more of the following Common Core State Standards © Copyright 2010. National Governors Association Center for Best Practices and Council of Chief State School Officers. All rights reserved. For more information about the Common Core State Standards, go to *http://www.corestandards.org/* or *http://www.teachercreated.com/standards/*.

Reading: Literature	Unit
Key Ideas and Details	
ELA.RL.3.1: Ask and answer questions to demonstrate understanding of a text, referring explicitly to the text as the basis for the answers.	Types of Writing: Narrative Vocabulary: Words and Phrases for Effect Figurative Language: Symbolism Figurative Language: Personification Figurative Language: Similes and Metaphors
ELA.RL.3.3: Describe characters in a story (e.g., their traits, motivations, or feelings) and explain how their actions contribute to the sequence of events.	Compound Sentences Types of Writing: Narrative Vocabulary: Words and Phrases for Effect Figurative Language: Personification
Craft and Structure	
ELA.RL.3.4: Determine the meaning of words and phrases as they are used in a text, distinguishing literal from nonliteral language.	Vocabulary: Words and Phrases for Effect Figurative Language: Similes and Metaphors Figurative Language: Alliteration and Onomatopoeia Figurative Language: Hyperbole
ELA.RL.3.5: Refer to parts of stories, dramas, and poems when writing or speaking about a text, using terms such as chapter, scene, and stanza; describe how each successive part builds on earlier sections.	Compound Sentences Capitalization: Titles Types of Writing: Narrative Figurative Language: Symbolism Figurative Language: Personification Figurative Language: Similes and Metaphors Figurative Language: Alliteration and Onomatopoeia
ELA.RL.3.6: Distinguish their own point of view from that of the narrator or those of the characters.	Types of Writing: Opinion

Reading: Informational Text	Unit
Key Ideas and Details	
ELA.RI.3.1: Ask and answer questions to demonstrate understanding of a text, referring explicitly to the text as the basis for the answers.	Pronouns: Subject and Object Conjunctions: Subordinating Punctuation: Possessives Types of Writing: Informative Vocabulary: Context Clues
ELA.RI.3.2: Determine the main idea of a text; recount the key details and explain how they support the main idea.	Conjunctions: Subordinating
ELA.RI.3.3: Describe the relationship between a series of historical events, scientific ideas or concepts, or steps in technical procedures in a text, using language that pertains to time, sequence, and cause/effect.	Conjunctions: Coordinating Conjunctions: Subordinating
Craft and Structure	
ELA.RI.3.4: Determine the meaning of general academic and domain-specific words and phrases in a text relevant to a *grade 3 topic or subject area*.	Vocabulary: Context Clues
Integration of Knowledge and Ideas	
ELA.RI.3.8: Describe the logical connection between particular sentences and paragraphs in a text (e.g., comparison, cause/effect, first/second/third in a sequence).	Conjunctions: Subordinating Run-on Sentences and Sentence Fragments Vocabulary: Context Clues

Writing	Unit
Text Types and Purposes	
ELA.W.3.1: Write opinion pieces on topics or texts, supporting a point of view with reasons.	Adjectives: Comparative and Superlative Adverbs: Comparative and Superlative Conjunctions: Subordinating Types of Writing: Opinion Formal and Informal English Vocabulary: Root Words and Prefixes Vocabulary: Root Words and Suffixes
ELA.W.3.2: Write informative/explanatory texts to examine a topic and convey ideas and information clearly.	Pronouns: Subject and Object Subject-Verb Agreement Conjunctions: Coordinating Run-on Sentences and Sentence Fragments Punctuation: Possessives Types of Writing: Informative Vocabulary: Root Words and Prefixes Vocabulary: Root Words and Suffixes Figurative Language: Analogies

Meeting Standards (cont.)

Writing (cont.)	Unit
Text Types and Purposes (cont.)	
ELA.W.3.3: Write narratives to develop real or imagined experiences or events using effective technique, descriptive details, and clear event sequences.	Verbs: Simple Past, Present, and Future Adjectives: Comparative and Superlative Compound Sentences Types of Writing: Narrative Vocabulary: Synonyms and Antonyms Vocabulary: Words and Phrases for Effect Vocabulary: Shades of Meaning Figurative Language: Idioms Figurative Language: Personification Figurative Language: Analogies
Production and Distribution of Writing	
ELA.W.3.4: With guidance and support from adults, produce writing in which the development and organization are appropriate to task and purpose.	*all*
ELA.W.3.5: With guidance and support from peers and adults, develop and strengthen writing as needed by planning, revising, and editing.	Verbs: Simple Past, Present, and Future Subject-Verb Agreement Conjunctions: Coordinating Conjunctions: Subordinating Complex Sentences Run-on Sentences and Sentence Fragments Punctuation: Possessives Punctuation: Dialogue Types of Writing: Informative Types of Writing: Narrative Figurative Language: Idioms Figurative Language: Symbolism Figurative Language: Personification Figurative Language: Similes and Metaphors Figurative Language: Alliteration and Onomatopoeia Figurative Language: Hyperbole
Research to Build and Present Knowledge	
ELA.W.3.7: Conduct short research projects that build knowledge about a topic.	Pronouns: Subject and Object Subject-Verb Agreement Conjunctions: Coordinating Conjunctions: Subordinating Run-on Sentences and Sentence Fragments Punctuation: Addresses Punctuation: Possessives Types of Writing: Informative Formal and Informal English Vocabulary: Root Words and Suffixes Vocabulary: Context Clues
ELA.W.3.8: Recall information from experiences or gather information from print and digital sources; take brief notes on sources and sort evidence into provided categories.	Pronouns: Subject and Object Adverbs: Comparative and Superlative Conjunctions: Coordinating Run-on Sentences and Sentence Fragments Punctuation: Possessives Types of Writing: Informative Formal and Informal English Vocabulary: Context Clues

Speaking & Listening	Unit
Comprehension and Collaboration	
ELA.SL.3.1: Engage effectively in a range of collaborative discussions (one-on-one, in groups, and teacher-led) with diverse partners on *grade 3 topics and texts,* building on others' ideas and expressing their own clearly.	*all*
ELA.SL.3.2: Determine the main ideas and supporting details of a text read aloud or information presented in diverse media and formats, including visually, quantitatively, and orally.	Figurative Language: Personification
ELA.SL.3.3: Ask and answer questions about information from a speaker, offering appropriate elaboration and detail.	Pronouns: Subject and Object Formal and Informal English Vocabulary: Root Words and Prefixes Figurative Language: Symbolism Figurative Language: Analogies

Meeting Standards _(cont.)_

Speaking & Listening _(cont.)_	Unit
Presentation of Knowledge and Ideas	
ELA.SL.3.4: Report on a topic or text, tell a story, or recount an experience with appropriate facts and relevant, descriptive details, speaking clearly at an understandable pace.	Pronouns: Subject and Object Adjectives: Comparative and Superlative Compound Sentences Punctuation: Dialogue Types of Writing: Opinion Vocabulary: Synonyms and Antonyms Figurative Language: Idioms
ELA.SL.3.5: Create engaging audio recordings of stories or poems that demonstrate fluid reading at an understandable pace; add visual displays when appropriate to emphasize or enhance certain facts or details.	Adjectives: Comparative and Superlative Punctuation: Dialogue Types of Writing: Opinion Figurative Language: Alliteration and Onomatopoeia
ELA.SL.3.6: Speak in complete sentences when appropriate to task and situation in order to provide requested detail or clarification.	_all_

Language	Unit
Conventions of Standard English	
ELA.L.3.1: Demonstrate command of the conventions of standard English grammar and usage when writing or speaking.	Nouns: Plural, Regular and Irregular Pronouns: Subject and Object Verbs: Simple Past, Present, and Future Subject-Verb Agreement Adjectives: Comparative and Superlative Adverbs: Comparative and Superlative Conjunctions: Coordinating Conjunctions: Subordinating Simple Sentences Compound Sentences Complex Sentences Run-on Sentences and Sentence Fragments Vocabulary: Root Words and Suffixes Vocabulary: Multiple-Meaning Words
ELA.L.3.2: Demonstrate command of the conventions of standard English capitalization, punctuation, and spelling when writing.	_all_
Knowledge of Language	
ELA.L.3.3: Use knowledge of language and its conventions when writing, speaking, reading, or listening.	_all_
Vocabulary Acquisition and Use	
ELA.L.3.4: Determine or clarify the meaning of unknown and multiple-meaning words and phrases based on grade 3 reading and content, choosing flexibly from a range of strategies.	Vocabulary: Words and Phrases for Effect Vocabulary: Root Words and Prefixes Vocabulary: Root Words and Suffixes Vocabulary: Context Clues Vocabulary: Multiple-Meaning Words Vocabulary: Shades of Meaning
ELA.L.3.5: Demonstrate understanding of figurative language, word relationships and nuances in word meanings.	Simple Sentences Punctuation: Dialogue Types of Writing: Opinion Types of Writing: Narrative Vocabulary: Words and Phrases for Effect Vocabulary: Shades of Meaning Figurative Language: Idioms Figurative Language: Symbolism Figurative Language: Personification Figurative Language: Similes and Metaphors Figurative Language: Analogies Figurative Language: Alliteration and Onomatopoeia Figurative Language: Hyperbole
ELA.L.3.6: Acquire and use accurately grade-appropriate conversational general academic, and domain-specific words and phrases, including those that signal spatial and temporal relationships (e.g., _After dinner that night we went looking for them_).	_all_